NO MORE
AVERAGE

Overcome an Average Life
and Live as The Real You

Andy Audate

First Edition

Names may have been changed to protect the identity of that individual. Mention of specific companies, authorities, or organizations in this book does not imply endorsement by the Author, nor does mention of specific companies, authorities, or organizations imply that they endorse this book or the Author.

For permissions contact:

AndyAudate@gmail.Com

Cover Design by Lisaarts
Cover Photo by Alexander Golovyrin Photography

NO MORE AVERAGE

Overcome an Average Life
and Live as The Real You

#NoMoreAverage

Andy Audate

To those who know they weren't meant to be average.
I understand you...

CONTENTS

Audiobook Available

www.AndyAudate.com

ONE-ON-ONE COACHING

TAKE YOUR LIFE & YOUR BUSINESS TO THE NEXT LEVEL

ANDYAUDATE@GMAIL.COM

PHONE: (323) 673-8876

INTRODUCTION

You are on your deathbed, lying down with your eyes glued to the ceiling. Literally, you are old, wrinkled and on your deathbed with your eyes glued to the ceiling. Death is around the corner; any minute, hour, or day now, it is soon to be your time.

What is the conversation you have with yourself? It is based on one of the two: you realized you lived your life as The Real You or you lived your life as The Unfulfilled You.

Were the responsibilities you had for your life met? And when I talk about responsibilities, I am not talking about your responsibility to pay your rent, or to hand in the homework or your duty to pay-off the mortgage or your obligation to have life insurance for those you are leaving behind. I am talking about the responsibility of not being average. Believe it or not, you living your life as The Real You is greater than any responsibility you can think of.

Your choice to follow averageness is the ultimate life choice you can make. Your choice to adhere to averageness is you committing extended spiritual suicide, which is spiritual suicide by your choices now and the effects taking place later. Even if you don't have kids now, the choice you make today, to be average or not, will affect your children's life, it will affect your mom and your dad's life, it will affect your significant other's life, it will affect a stranger's life, and not only will it affect your life as well, but your choice could either be the reason someone lives or someone is not alive. Don't over think this, this is common sense but overlooked, it'll be explained in subsequent chapters.

When on an airplane, during the pre-flight safety announcement, in the event of an in-flight emergency, airplane flight attendants advise you to fit your oxygen mask on prior to helping people needing help, such as children, or the disabled. If you don't do this, you cannot help other people, as you will lose oxygen.

The Real You is screaming "Save Yourself." Before you can save anyone else from averageness; you must save yourself. Your life has a purpose and there are people who depend on the completion of your life's purpose.

Your life's responsibility depends on one choice, and one choice only, whether you decide to save yourself and not be average, or not save yourself and be average. This book will aid you in taking the next step to living life as The Real You, the best version of you.

1

IT BEGINS WITH A THOUGHT

"No truly great person ever thought themselves so."
— William Hazlitt

L ooking in the bathroom mirror with my fists clenched, my eyebrows contracted and my teeth showing like a dog does to show aggression, I'm looking right into my reflection's eyes and I yell as loud as I can "I am not average! I am not average! I am not average!" I was angry and exhausted because I knew the life I was living was not the life meant for me and I have been in my own way. I have a duty to actualize my thoughts-of-greatness.

My mom and dad are relying on me; my neighbor is depending on me; my future kids, my little brother and my future wife are relying on me; the kids in my old neighborhood, who are shooting each other because of boredom and other nonsense, they are depending on me;

my future self is depending on me; every single person that I have ever said anything positive to is relying on me; the person sitting across from me at this Starbucks as I write this book is depending on me. I cannot fail, do you see how many people are depending on me? Many of these individuals do not know they are relying on me. My level of success has not yet been met for them to be aware.

When I say dependent on me, I do not sense I am superior than anyone or I am proud that countless people depend on me. The responsibility has been given to me (through thought) and I have accepted. Understand what I am saying with an open mind. Society attempts to have us live with a closed mind and live a life of averageness; I wrote this book because I was sick! Sick of averageness and sick of it consuming my life!

I was sick of averageness consuming the mind of people around me and it could be consuming your mind and life. Average qualities were in my life unbeknownst me, I had no idea that I was average. I thought life was supposed to be like that, then I learned about thoughts-of-greatness and being the real version of myself.

Be Happy in All You Do

The bible says in Ecclesiastes 3:12-13 NIV "I know that there is nothing better for people than to be happy and to do good while they live. That each of them may eat and drink, and find satisfaction in all their toil—this is the gift of God." I understand this as Toil being the work you do, and I am not talking about what your job is, I am talking about where and what your efforts are being spent on or how you live your life. There is no way you are here to work a job you dread going to everyday.

Les Brown, a renowned motivational speaker, once

said: "Statistics says, most people suffered their first major heart attack on Monday morning between 8 am and 9 am." Coincidently average people speak negatively about Monday morning because of its connection with going back to work from a short period of two days without work. You were not meant to live a life of dissatisfaction and hatred for the known five business days of the week. The five days of the week that many people hate, make up 71% of their life. You aren't given a life to live to dread 71% of it. **We are meant to find and have satisfaction in all of that we do.**

One characteristic of averageness is complaining without doing anything about it. You have the ability to make a choice! You can make decisions for yourself! Do not hate your job, complain about it and not do a single thing to make a change.

Don't get sick of your job; get sick of your choice to continually keep going and doing something that is causing negativity in your life. Now, I'm aware there are positions and jobs that can help you in achieving your goals and that's not what I am talking about. I am talking to the person who wakes up in the morning, every morning, sighs with dissatisfaction, and never once looked forward to their day as if he or she didn't have a choice.

Actualize Your Thoughts-of-Greatness

What makes me happy is progress. I work to progress daily and that is what keeps a smile on my face. I believe that is a human trait, happiness comes from the continuation of getting better daily. In this chapter, the definition of Better is the progression towards your goals.

Thought(s)-of-greatness is defined as an idea or feeling produced in the mind, which is parallel or an abstract direction to your definition of success.

Imagine someone or some people who impacted your life in a positive way. For them to be in the position to impact your life; in most cases, they would have had to go through a process of development, which usually starts with a thought-of-greatness.

My parents impacted my life, the two people that gave me life, my parents, they are both immigrants; they impacted my life by giving me the opportunity to live.

I know this sounds so simple but what it took for my parents to meet and create me was much more than simple. They both were born in Haiti and didn't meet each other until they came to the United States in their 20s. The impact in my life besides the principles they instilled in me, was giving me life. The actualization of their thoughts-of-greatness led to me being a human on earth.

Haiti is a poor country but each of my parent's broke-through by not being average. They actualized their thoughts-of-greatness, then they met and dated, then they created me.

I went to my dad's hometown, Carice, Haiti about 2 years ago; for the first time, I got to see what life was like in Haiti; most importantly I got to see where my dad was raised. In Carice, Haiti, it is normal to be poor, that's average.

Andy in Carice, Haiti – October 2015

When I was there, I saw most people living under means that were less than homeless individuals living in the United States.

One man I met was wearing white female sneakers for children, so small, the front of the shoes was getting ready to tear open to expose his toes. Other men I met, either had sandals that did not fit their feet and were worn out or did not have shoes at all.

Many of the homes in my dad's hometown did not have electricity. When nighttime came, the city went completely dark with no electricity besides one streetlight that was on for the entire city. There were a small handful of homes that were fortunate to have generators to power their homes but the average, the norm, was to live without electricity. Understand the averageness in this area was to live in third world conditions.

Before my dad came to the United States, he had not met my mom. Before my dad came to the United States, he had no idea his first child born in the U.S. would be a boy and he would name him Andy. Before my dad came, he had no idea of how many lives he can positively influence back in Haiti by his decision to move. Before my dad came, he had no idea of how many people he would motivate in the United States. My dad is now a respiratory therapist and before he came to the United States, he had no idea of how many American lives he would save.

Because of the actions my dad took to not be average in his hometown, it allowed him to attain and maintain the resources to provide for the people that are short of necessary resources, like food, money, water, and shelter. When I was in Haiti, my cousin told me that my dad pays for him and his brother's schooling and their books. The payment is on a recurring monthly basis.

Had my dad stayed in Haiti and not leave in search of actualizing his thoughts-of-greatness, it is very likely my dad wouldn't have the resources to provide for my cousin's school and schoolbooks.

On a weekly basis, my dad gets phone calls from people in Haiti requesting loans or donations and my dad is able to provide funds for those loans and donations, but had my dad stayed in Haiti, he wouldn't have the ability to provide. Had my dad stayed in Haiti and live average, it is likely you would not be reading this book, therefore my dad had a responsibility to you that he followed his thought-of-greatness, to give you the opportunity to read this book.

Had my dad stayed in Haiti, it is very unlikely that the people I have motivated and inspired so far would not have been motivated and inspired.

Before my dad could take part in conceiving his first son, he had a responsibility to not be average in his circumstance and he had to accept the responsibility to put himself in the position to take part in my creation. My life depended on it, literally! My dad had a responsibility to my little brother to take part in creating him. Prior to my dad being able to put himself in a position to do any of these things, he had to save himself from being average.

The Real Him was him telling himself to actualize his thoughts-of-greatness, and he listened.

Before you can save anyone else, you must save yourself. Before my cousin was born, my dad had a responsibility to be able to pay for his schooling and school books. Understand the emphasis on able. Having to and being able to, are two different types of responsibilities. My dad doesn't have to pay for my cousin's school, my dad is able to pay and he chooses to.

All of this began with a thought. It began with my dad's thoughts-of-greatness; which was him being a citizen of the United States, and doing whatever he must do to provide for himself, his then soon to be family, and the people he left in Haiti, to actualize his thoughts-of-greatness. My dad knew and had a thought that he was not average, and he accepted the responsibility to do whatever it would take to turn his thoughts-of-greatness into reality.

You may be having thoughts-of-greatness, this book is to have you realize that the thoughts-of-greatness you have are not accidental and you need to act on it. You have a responsibility not only to yourself but to other people, including individuals you may not have met yet. You have a responsibility of not being average.

If you thought I was selfish because I assumed a responsibility of so many people, based on their dependence on me, stop that! I am focused on making sure my thoughts-of-greatness become a reality to provide for countless people.

What is Average?

Average is defined as living vicariously through, or mimicking the efforts and ideas of other people. The thoughts you have been having about your future and the life you are supposed to live are not in your mind by accident. Those thoughts are your navigational map for your life and your mind is the navigating platform.

If you follow the directions of your thoughts-of-greatness, you will be fulfilled, as this is the fulfillment of your dreams and aspirations.

If you do not follow the directions of your thoughts-of-greatness, you may be one of the individuals that lay on a deathbed with self-talk that is aligned with living life as The Unfulfilled You.

Dissatisfaction within yourself and difficulties with the attainment of living life as The Real You arise by unforeseeable circumstances, negative emotions, limiting beliefs and when you allow other people to dictate your life either by their indirect influence or verbal directions that are in misalignment with your thoughts-of-greatness. Indirect influencers are individuals that influence and sway you into a direction either aligned with your goals or in most cases, not aligned with your goals, this is done without verbally telling you what to do.

This person could be a family member, acquaintance, friend, mentor or stranger. The way they influence you can come from many ways if the person is not giving you commands for what you should or need to do. An indirect influence does not necessarily have to come from someone speaking to you; it can come from being around an individual and there is something that you are intrigued by. And this thing that intrigues you, influences you to do or follow that interest.

An indirect influence can also be done verbally (without commands or concise directions), physical movements, and non-verbal communication. Verbal directors are individuals that tell you specifically what to do by verbally directing you (with commands and concise directions).

An example of an influence (verbal director) is your mom telling you to go to college, get a degree in the medical field, and be a doctor and that is not aligned with your thoughts-of-greatness. If you allow her indirect influence or verbal directions, that counteract your thoughts-of-greatness, to enter your mind, you will become imbalanced. This is partly because a portion of you wants to progress, be better and be fulfilled from your thoughts-of-greatness, but the other part is adhering to the indirect influence or verbal direction of another person, which is the reason for the imbalance.

In the previous example, if your mom told you to go to

college, get a degree in the medical field and be a doctor the rest of your life but you want to be an entrepreneur and start multiple businesses in different industries. There will be an imbalance because you cannot simultaneously do both; you must go one of the two ways. This is an example and can be understood in all walks of life as well as occupations. The imbalance can happen in your school, your job, your marriage, etc. If The Real You wants something, and the other part of you adheres to another person's indirect influence or verbal direction in your life, you will be imbalanced; you are human and can only go in one direction.

When not handled in the right amount of time, the effects of being imbalanced can result in the lack of actualizing your thoughts-of-greatness, idleness, procrastination, suicide, death, complacency; the indulging into drugs, partying, alcohol, sex, addiction and other negative tendencies.

You Can Make a Decision

97% of people have the ability to make decisions for themselves and know exactly what they want to happen in their life or in the next chapter in their life. When you feel, you have no direction and don't know what to do; it is not because of the lack of direction, it is because of an imbalance.

You may be consciously aware of your imbalance; or which is usually the case, you may not be aware of it at all, and understand it as cluelessness. This happens often due to your choice to adhere to the indirect influencers in your life, and/or verbal directors in your life for a long duration of time.

If you perceive you do not have thoughts-of-greatness or have not figured out your thoughts-of-greatness, but you know you want better for your life and you just do not know what to do; indirect influencers in your life, or verbal directors can advise in getting you started to figure out your thoughts-of-greatness or figuring out exactly what you do not want.

Dependent on the information this individual is giving you, the relationship with either one of the two influencers: Verbal Directors and Indirect Influencers can be beneficial or harmful to your success.

Remember there are two types of influencers, **Verbal Directors** and **Indirect Influencers**. Advice from indirect influencers in your life and/or verbal directors guide you on a path that you may or may not want to take.

For your understanding, in subsequent chapters, I will be going to go into detail of my life of how indirect influencers and verbal directors aided me in figuring out my thoughts of greatness and what happened after. Additionally, you will understand how to figure out your thoughts-of-greatness and become The Real You.

2

SLEEPING GIANT

*"I fear all we have done is to awaken a sleeping giant
and fill him with a terrible resolve."*

–Isoruku Yamamoto

November 2016, Hollywood, California, I am at a birthday party bash. At the party, a friend of mine came to me in awe asking me if I am really writing a book. I looked at him and smiled and said, "yeah, I'm writing a book." With a smirk on my face, I also tell him a few months prior, God put a book launch on my mind and it's been on my heart ever since. I believe part of my purpose on this earth is to encourage people to step in faith and start actualizing their thoughts-of-greatness. Writing and self-publishing this book was one of my thoughts-of-greatness!

At the party, he asked me how many pages have I written so far and I told him I wasn't done with the first page but the book will be finished in January. He looked at me with disbelief and a smirk on his face; he said, "January? Are you sure you're going to be finished in January? That's like three months from now." I let him know with confidence, "I'll be done in January! I'm good with deadlines" and I shook his hand.

I added I am in the pre-order stage and he can pre-order the book on my website. He asked me how many preorders do I have. This question stumped me and I will tell you why… I answered his question by beating around the bush. I said "I'm going in blinded; you know how you post an Instagram picture and wait until the next day to find out how many likes it got, I'm in the same boat.

I'm going to grab a drink though." That question stumped me because I had zero pre-orders and I hyped the crap out of this book on my Instagram page (@CantQuitAndy). And because I have zero pre-orders, it simply makes me feel like a failure! Therefore, I didn't want to answer the question directly and I got out of the situation by going to get a drink.

I've been thinking about that conversation with my friend and he has no idea, but he awoke a sleeping giant in me. However, this conversation isn't the first time the sleeping giant has been awoken in me. Throughout my life, there have been a few incidents the sleeping giant inside of me has been awoken. And one situation that comes to mind is when I had to decide to expand my business; that will be coming in a subsequent chapter. More importantly though, this wasn't the first time I set an unrealistic goal and someone doubted me.

Now I know he had some concerns and I'm sure he wondered is it possible to accomplish that task of writing a book in such a short period of time, as the average time period for a book completion can take anywhere from six months to three years, I have less than 90 days! The task and period of time to complete the task was abnormal, therefore it is easy to question my work ethic, but all I could do was look at him with the thought going through my mind that I Am Not Average.

Who is Andy Audate?

My name is Audate (Awe-Date). Andy Audate! My mom, pregnant at the time was watching Oprah early in the morning, Gush! Her water broke. My aunt, who was in the house with my mom at the time, went down the stairs with my mom, helped her in the passenger side of the car, went around the other side to the driver seat, started it and began to drive my mom to the hospital. My mom, in the passenger seat was calm, cool, and collective about the fact she was in labor. My aunt on the other hand, panicked and drove frantically.

She went nuts asking questions like "What do I do? Are you okay? What's going on?" Being that my mom was calm, cool, and collective. My mom swapped seats with my aunt and decided to drive herself to the hospital. This must be where I get my calmness, coolness, and collectiveness from when I am in situations of disarray.

I took my first breath on Saturday, New Year's Eve morning in Boston, Massachusetts. At 6:42 AM, a beautiful light skin baby boy was born. This baby boy was so light; he was placed under a special light for the next 24 hours to correct his skin tone. That once light skin baby boy is the handsome man you see on the cover of this book. Seven years later, I moved from Massachusetts to the gritty streets of Central Falls, Rhode Island.

I went to school at the local catholic middle school, Saint Elizabeth Ann Seton Academy. I was an outcast in school; I was different than the other kids. My peers didn't accept me easily and I coped with it by creating attention for myself by becoming the class clown. Being the class clown had its perks and its disadvantages. One of the perks was I had people around me that I could make smile and laugh and a disadvantage was I was in trouble often.

Two years later, I am now nine years old, I move from Central Falls to Pawtucket, Rhode Island. Central Falls was too violent and I'm sure there was other grown up affairs with my parents that I wasn't aware of at the time. Fourth grade is when I started my journey of entrepreneurship. Now I live in Pawtucket, Rhode Island, I transferred schools. I became a student of St. Leo, short for Saint Leo The Great School, another catholic K-12 Grade school.

Leader and a Student

I was an obnoxious student. I was obnoxious to my teachers; but to my peers, I was the funny-cool guy. Being I was different and didn't fit in, I got attention by making kids around me laugh. To further explain how I was different: I didn't like what other kids liked.

For example, the other kids watched cartoons on TV, I watched "America's Most Wanted." The other kids played video games in their spare time; I watched videos on different topics such as life in prison and reality shows. There was little to nothing I can do to connect with my peers besides laughter, and it usually involved me doing ridiculous things to make them laugh.

Not only did I make the kids laugh, I was also a leader and that made the teacher resent me a little more since I had a little-bit of control of how the class behaved. I remember one of my teachers pulling me aside and letting me know I am a leader and what I do, the other kids follow. The teacher asked me politely to behave in class, I usually didn't comply, and I did my own thing.

Some say leaders are created, which may be true in some cases; but in my case, I was a natural born leader, leading my third, fourth, and fifth grade class. When I was living in Massachusetts, my uncle Mike, who was my role model, gave me advice, which to this day I still live by, he said "Don't be a follower, be a leader." I was younger than seven years old when he told me that, and that quote remains a principle of mine.

Mom's Dream

It was in my fourth-grade year, when my mom and dad opened a boutique that sold dental hygiene products and uniforms for medical field employees. Individuals such as doctors, respiratory therapists, hygienists, medical assistants, dental assistants and anyone who wore scrubs would come to my parent's boutique to buy scrubs and their shoes for work. It was my mom's dream her store, G & B Uniforms and Dental Shop be a success. She worked so hard day-in and day-out to make it successful.

She had everyone in my immediate family help-out somehow. My dad helped by manning the store when my mom wasn't working. My little brother, Alain, helped by keeping the store clean when he was there. I was a sales associate and I was left alone to do sales at times when no adult was at the store. I could be there since there was little to no foot traffic. My mom had one store and that store changed locations two times.

The first location was strategically placed half a mile away from my school, St. Leo. It had two large clear glass windows in the front of the store with a clear glass door in the middle of the two clear glass windows.

This location was a stand-alone commercial building on the first floor and residential on the second and third floor.

The actual store was 1000 square feet in the front end, and the back end was 300 square feet. When you walk into the store from the sidewalk, you walked into a grey-carpeted store with racks and racks of clothes.

The shoes were placed throughout the store and there were shoes on the wall to my left and the wall to the right. In the back of the store, behind a dangling curtain in a doorway without a door that separated the front end to the "employees only" back end was a bathroom, a yellow wooden desk and a sink. I took over that yellow desk.

I organized that desk with a Rolodex, pens, and other supplies. I used the desk to do homework but I wanted to use the desk to do more important things. I didn't know what exactly I wanted to do, but I wanted to be responsible for something and utilize that desk and my time while I was in the store.

Since the store was less than half a mile away, after-school, I walked to the store daily. I asked my mom to give me some responsibility in the store but it was hard for her to do since I was only nine years old. In my mind, at nine years old, I felt like I was an adult. I was always older in my mind than what my birth certificate said. She did give me a little bit of responsibility. She had me write numbers on stickers to price the clothes and shoes, throw paper away and simple tasks like that.

However, I wanted to do something much more important than that. I was thinking about running a Department in the store. At nine years old you can see where my mind was at, I wanted to have my own Department that I oversaw in my mom's store, but I had no idea what I would do. There was little to no foot traffic at the first store; we moved the store to another location.

The second location was much smaller; it was 600 square feet and that yellow desk was gone. There went my dreams of having my own department in the store. The

Second store was part of a strip of different stores and boutiques. The new location was located about a mile away from my school now on a busier Street. The busier Street should bring more foot traffic to the store, so I thought.

In the strip of stores and boutiques, at the end was a restaurant called Kip's. This restaurant was the neighborhood spot for everyone to eat. They sold wieners and burgers and so much more. After school, I would want to get food but I didn't have money to buy it. My mom was struggling with the business, all the help I gave in the store was unpaid. Kip's had the best wieners and I was frustrated because I wanted to eat food at Kip's but my mom would usually make me wait to go home to eat.

You know how moms are, you want food and their response is "wait until we get home." Not only did I want money to buy food but also I wanted money to gain my own independence. Yes, at nine years old, I wanted independence to buy what I wanted, when I wanted.

First Job

Next to my mom's new store location was a barbershop, Kingdom Cutz owned and operated by a gentleman named Scott. Scott was my barber. The shop had four barbers and four barber stations and one hair washing station. In the first station, Scott claimed his station by placing his equipment on the table in front of the mirror.

Scott rented out the remaining barber stations. In the second station was where Bob placed his equipment. In the third, Sam was the barber in that station. And the fourth is where John worked. Any barber could use the hair washing station.

I was getting bored sitting down and wasting time at my mom's store, on top of that, I wanted to make some money and there wasn't money that I could make at my mom's store. Since Scott was my barber and I had a barber-client relationship with him, I asked him if I could work for him. I told him I would sweep the hair off the floor, clean the bathroom and get him and the other barbers food from Kip's when they wanted it. Scott accepted and he hired me.

He made me feel official when he gave a red barber cape. I felt more official when I was getting paid $5 per hour. At nine years, old, that is a lot of money, especially when I was working 25 to 30 hours weekly.

I would go to school in the morning, walk to my mom's store after school, drop off my bag at the store and go straight to Kingdom Cutz to work. I was making my own money; I was in love with that idea. I loved having that cash in my hand and in my pocket. I loved the sound it made when I took it out of my pocket, swoosh-swoosh! I would sometimes count my money, put it in my pocket; take my money out and recount it for no reason at all, and I could finally go to Kip's and buy a wiener without asking my mom for money, I did that often.

I swept the hair off the floor, cleaned the bathroom and got Scott and the other barbers food from Kip's when they wanted it for about six months. After six months, I was getting money but I wanted more, I wanted more responsibility and more importance in the shop. I asked Scott to teach me how to cut hair. Since I was already spending a lot of time in the shop and I was getting older, cutting hair was part of the journey.

Capitalize on the Opportunity

Scott slowly started to show me how to cut men's hair. There are different strokes with the clippers and it is dependent on the hair type; there are different types of clippers and there are different times when to use them. He began teaching me the basics of hair cutting. There were a few times the customer's hair would be dirty or they had gel in their hair and the customer's hair had to be washed with water and soap in the hair washing station.

It was rare that a customer's hair had to be washed, but Scott taught me how to wash hair anyway. After I got the hang of hair washing, Scott eventually delegated the task of washing the customer's hair to me, when a customer's hair needed to be washed, I would take them to the hair washing station and wash their hair, this was rare though.

I was adding responsibility to my job description and giving myself more importance in the shop. I was the sweeper, bathroom cleaner, food fetcher and occasional hair washer. I noticed that people liked when I washed their hair before they got a haircut.

I presented the idea to Scott that I make the hair washing station, my own station and every customer that came into the shop would get a hair wash before their haircut. It made sense to me since customers were waiting ten minutes to an hour in the waiting lounge to get a haircut.

In addition to the $5 per hour I was making from Scott, I was making tips from the people I was washing hair for. As I was the hair washer in the shop, Scott was still teaching me how to cut hair but I had yet to cut someone's hair.

What my uncle told me about being a leader always stuck in my head, and I had to take charge of what I wanted to do, I was eager to learn and make more money by cutting hair. For my first haircut, I convinced my little brother, Alain, to allow me to cut his hair. He was reluctant to let me touch his hair, but I was able to convince him.

Plus, it was beneficial for my mom since she didn't

have to pay for his haircut. Alain usually gets a fade on the side and that's what I was going to give him. A fade is an ethnic haircut where the hair at the bottom portion of the head is as close as possible to the skin and the hair blends to any length at the top. I saw Scott do this haircut hundreds of times before and I got the haircutting basics down, it's my turn to try.

I put Alain in the chair, and I put the cape on him, to protect hair from sticking to his clothes, and on his body. I am amped up and excited at this moment. I have a smirk on my face because I am trying hard to hide my huge grin. Alain is sitting in the chair as if it is another haircut, so his emotion is no different than any other haircut. But my swagger and confidence is high at this point. In the back of my head I am a little nervous, what if I mess up? I grab a clipper, put the 0-attachment on the clipper and start cutting his hair.

A clipper is a motor with two separate serrated blades that goes back and forth. The back and forth motion of the two separate serrated blades is what cuts the hair. When the clipper is attached to an attachment, the attachment adds length to the clipper giving the clipper a greater distance from the scalp, cutting less hair as the attachment size grows. Each attachment has a different size that is represented by a number, the higher the number, the longer the hair will be from the scalp.

A 0-attachment will get very close to the scalp showing the pores of the head. A 1-attachment is a little bit higher, a 2-attachment is a little higher than a 1-attachment, a 3-attachment is a little higher from the 2-attachment and so on. For visual purpose, the 1-attachment would bring hair length to about the size of the hair on my arm.

In Alain's haircut, he was going to have a 0-attachment on the side and a 2-attachement on top of his head. When doing a fade, there is a technique of bringing the hair at the bottom portion of the head from 0-attachment and blending the hair to the top to a 2. The keyword is blend. Since I was new, I knew the theory but I didn't know how to apply the technique and I gave Alain a hard line in the middle of his head from a 0-attachment to a 2-attachment without blending. The other barbers at the barbershop called it a bowl. I was embarrassed that I did the haircut wrong. Scott had to fix it.

I figured the problem was the blending technique; I didn't know how to blend the hair. It would be a few weeks until I got my second chance at cutting someone's hair. In the meantime, I kept focus on what Scott did. I had a keen eye on how Scott cut hair and I asked a lot of questions. Not only did I focus on Scott's technique, I also learned from Bob, Sam and John. Bob had a more relaxed approach in comparison to how Scott cut hair.

Scott was tight when cutting hair, Bob leaned back. John didn't want to show me much; he was more focused on making his money. Sam was odd in his technique and how he interacted with the other people in the shop overall. Sam's techniques were quick and get the customer out of the chair as soon as possible. Scott focused on having great customer service.

Scott's customer service was so great; there was this one occurrence where a man came into the shop just as we were about to close. This man was bald with a button up shirt and slacks. In my thoughts, I questioned what is it that he wanted since he was bald, there was no hair to cut. He told Scott that his wife was out of town and he couldn't shave his back and wanted Scott to do it for him. I started to laugh and thought this was a joke.

On the other hand, Scott shrugged his shoulders and agreed to do it. The customer took off his shirt and pulled out a razor and said "I brought a razor so you don't have to use your equipment". Scott used the customer's razor to shave his back, which I have never seen before. It took Scott no more than 10 minutes to shave the hair off the customer's back.

When he was done, the customer offered Scott money and Scott declined. Scott told the customer not to worry about it. The customer walked away with a pleased look on his face. That 10 minutes turned this customer into a lifelong raving fan of Kingdom Cutz and over time should refer people to the shop, expanding the business.

I got my chance to cut another person's hair when a white guy came in; he had to be not a day over fourteen years old. I felt at that time I had learned enough on the haircutting technique besides blending. I did not know how to blend a fade, and still to this day, I still do not know how to blend a fade. When the customer walked in, Scott was eating lunch, I asked Scott to cut that customer's hair and Scott would still get the money from the customer; I just wanted the experience. Scott gave me the green light and said "yeah, that's fine."

The customer was about 5 feet 5 inches tall, Caucasian with long-blonde hair and a pointy nose that looked like he can smell anything within 10 feet from him; his nose was always pointed in the direction his face was facing. He wore baggy jeans and a plain white t-shirt.

I walked up to him and said "are you here for a haircut?" he replied, "yeah," I gave him an up and down nod while waving my hand in the direction towards me as I walked over to the barber station to prepare a seat for him to sit in. I asked what type of haircut did he want and he said he wanted to get "a 1 all-around." When he said 1, it meant that he wanted a 1-attachment, and all-around meant that the 1-attachment would be used to cut hair from the crown of the head (top), both sides of the temple and the back of the head, no blending was involved.

It was a pretty easy haircut and I was excited but my

face had an expression of confusion because his hair was long. To bring his long hair to a size 1, a lot of hair would be cut off and that was uncommon for a white person. This is the first time I have seen this customer in the shop and I was not sure if "a 1 all-around" meant something else in another barbershop. I asked him multiple times if he was sure that he wanted a 1, and he said yes every time.

But since I knew a 1-attachment was low, I told him I would start with a 3-attachment and work my way down. When I started cutting his hair with the 3-attachment, his face had a mixture of shock and disgust. He told me that the 3-attachment was too low. I had a smirk on my face because he previously asked for a 1. The smirk was out of relief and not out of spitefulness. He would have been mad if I had given him what he asked for.

A line up is when the natural hairline of the temples, forehead, and back are shaved into sharp angles and straight lines. I was proficient with lining-up and I proceeded with the line up on this customer, I gave him a straight and fresh line up. The haircut came out good, and the customer agreed, the length was just his only concern.

I have a good memory to connect faces to occurrences in my past; I ended up seeing this guy a few years later at a party and reacquainted myself. He too recalled the situation and we laughed over it. What I learned from this is to be careful of what you ask for and to consider the details of what it is you're are asking for before deciding.

3

LEAD YOUR LIFE

"If you don't like something, change it. If you can't change it, change your attitude. Don't complain."

–Maya Angelou

Being a leader is more than having an influence on other people for them to do as you say. A characteristic of being a leader is the ability to control what is in your control. In life, there are things you have control over and there are things that you do not have control over. You must be able to control the controllable and be nimble to the things you don't have control over.

We don't have control over time but you have control over what you do with your time. One thing you do have control over is where you are and what you do with the time given to you. In my opinion, time is the most precious gift, it doesn't come tied with a bow but it's still a gift. Money and many tangible objects can be replaced but time can't be replaced. Once you lose a minute, you will never receive that back. You have 86,400 seconds in a day, that's 86,400 opportunities to work towards a goal and receive the reward you most desire.

Since time won't come back, when I was going to my mom's store after school every day, I was wasting time because I was not doing anything productive or anything that generated revenue. I knew that I wanted to do something important and make money; I took control over where I spent my time after school and I took control over what I did in that time.

I did this by going to Scott and asking him for a specific job that would be of use to him and would put money in my pocket. I swept, cleaned, washed hair and got the barbers food. This allowed the barbers to focus on cutting hair while I did their nanny tasks. Leading your life is being the boss of what you do with your time. Time is the most valuable gift you have; when time is spent, you cannot get it back. If I allowed myself to be led by the situation I was in, I would have sat in my mom's store, sulk over the fact that I had no money and be miserable with the time that I had.

Average people allow life to lead them, and they go with the flow. You may ask a friend how has their life been, and they say, "just been going with the flow." Metaphorically life is like you are in a kayak on the water.

The kayak represents your vehicle to complete your life's purpose; the water represents circumstances that you have no control over in your life. The paddle is a tool used for pushing against the water and it represents what you have control over. The shore represents an abundant life, or the ability to live and have esoteric experiences while you are alive because you can go on the shore and maneuver throughout the rest of the world.

Your ultimate goal in life should be to reach the shore also known as freedom and live that abundant life that allows you to maneuver throughout the world and have those esoteric experiences intended only for you, this is your thoughts-of-greatness.

To do this, you must use your paddle and work against the current that is attempting to bring you to the middle of the ocean where there is nothing but a copious amount of water that has no greater purpose in your life than to keep you in the middle of the ocean, until you die. However, the shore may not be seen from where you are in the ocean, but you must paddle with belief that you are headed towards the shore.

You are responsible for the kayak and where the kayak ends up. You are responsible for your being and where you end up (in life). Without taking action of paddling, the kayak will go wherever the current takes it, the kayak will drift. Where you are in life is dependent on if you paddle or not and the direction you paddle.

Paddle towards the shore and paddle stronger and harder than the water against you. Paddling is taking action with the things you have control over. I understand I was only nine years old at the time, but my thoughts were not of a nine-year-old child. I knew I wanted to make money. I used my brain and thought of ways to make money, and there came a thought-of-greatness, me working for Kingdom Cutz. There was a need since there was a lot of hair on the ground after each haircut and not enough time for the barbers to pick it up after each haircut.

The definition of lead is to "be in charge or command of." Lead your life; lead yourself with the time given to you. Where you are today, where you were yesterday and where you are going to be tomorrow are the sum decisions of your ability to lead your life. Control where you spend your time and what you do in that time.

4

YOUNG ENTREPRENEUR

"I may have been born like this, I may have been created to be like this, but I am who I am because I am like this."
                                                                    –Andy Audate

I was young but I was exposed to the boss life. My mom owned a shop and called the shots at the store. She wasn't an employee; she had employees. Being around Scott and my mom showed me that it is possible to be a business owner and showed me the most basic day-to-day operations of owning a small business.

I was "making money" working at the barbershop, which at the time was averaging no more than $150 per week, I had to deal with something most hourly workers deal with, lack of hours! Working at the barbershop, I was not able to get all the hours I wanted. What was once 25 to 30 hours weekly, quickly became 12 hours between Friday and Saturday. However, I still wanted to make money, so I had to come up with ideas to make money. I created different avenues to generate revenue from yard sales to lemonade stands, to shoveling snow to raking leaves.

The type of person I was and still am is a go-getter. What I want, I go and get; sometimes there are obstacles throughout the journey but regardless, I maneuver through them. I did not allow the lack of hours to negatively affect me. I had to strategize and come up with different avenues to generate revenue.

I use the word "revenue" because I looked at myself as a business. As a business that creates businesses and provide a service or product for people and in return the consumer of the service or product paid me money. I was using this terminology and understanding business before working at Kingdom Cutz.

From the point of view of standing on the sidewalk and looking at Kingdom Cutz from the outside of the shop, my mom's store was on the right of the barbershop. My mom was able to strike a deal with the landlord of the property and my mom then moved the store to the left side of the barbershop which that location was about two times bigger than the previous store and had a back room, which the then store didn't have a backroom.

The new location, which stood at 509 Armistice Blvd in Pawtucket, RI, was more spacious than the second location, and still in the same shopping strip allowing me to still work at the barbershop.

Since the new store would have a backroom and more space, I wanted to take advantage of that and I created a business within my mom's business. That dream of having my own department in the store didn't die with the lack of the yellow desk. As a business, manufactures of different products in thousands of different industries are available to you. Since G & B Uniforms and Dental Shop was a legitimate business, I had thousands of manufactures at my disposal to order their products to resell. My mom would provide the startup capital but I didn't know what products to buy.

Business Lesson

My mom taught me a valuable business lesson, manufactures produce items for businesses to resell. The manufacture gives businesses an incentive that when the business orders more units, the cost per unit will decrease and the profit to the manufacture for the entire order increases. This is a win-win for the business and the manufacture. Here is an example showing the profit to the manufacture when a business orders more units:

Manufacture Cost per Unit	Units Ordered (Qty)	Business Cost per Unit	Manufacture Profit for Order
	50	$2.00	$50
	100	$1.90	$90
$1.00	200	$1.80	$160
	300	$1.70	$210
	400	$1.60	$240

The cost the business pays per unit decreases as the unit quantity of the order increases. This is a win for the manufacture because their profit increases. This is a win for the business because when the business markups each product, their profit per unit increases since the cost per unit was decreased.

In the table below you will understand how a business makes profit in the example when they purchase more units.

Business Cost per Unit	Units Ordered (Qty)	Resell Price	Business Profit for Order	Profit Margin
$2.00	50		$100	50%
$1.90	100		$210	52.5%
$1.80	200	$4.00	$440	55%
$1.70	300		$690	57.5%
$1.60	400		$960	60%

My mom taught me the basic economics behind the relationship of a manufacture and a business. The business cost per unit is how much we, the business paid per unit. Knowing the economics, I had to figure out what type of product I will sell and what quantity I will start off with.

As I was figuring out what product to sell, my mom suggested that I sell novelty items, such as toys, plastic rings, jump ropes, etc. It made sense to me because when kids came into the store to shop with their parents, I was connecting with them but the kids had nothing to buy.

I followed my mom's suggestion; she retrieved and gave me a catalog of novelty toys that showed all the novelty items that was available for purchase. I reviewed the catalog and chose the items I wanted and the quantity. In this case, my mom was a verbal director, which would be part of the beginning of my entrepreneurship. My mom placed the order and fronted the money to buy the products for my business, Andy's Kid Shop.

I was impatiently waiting for the delivery of the package that would be the start of my business. I was waiting for a box, I wasn't sure how big the box would be; this box would contain the items that when sold, money would be in my pocket.

I am an over-thinker, and I thought about how the items I ordered were manufactured. I thought to myself that it was likely made in china, where majority of the world's novelty products are made. In the meantime, of fulfillment and shipment of the order, I would think about the interaction of my first sale. Asking myself "what will I do when a customer is in front of me?"

I came to my mom's store after school and asked my mom, "is the package here?" I did this every single day until the package arrived at the store. Can you imagine me awaiting the beginning of the following of my mom's footsteps and starting my own business? Thinking about ways I can expand Andy's Kid Shop. Should I have a sign in the store?

What if I put a large white-foldable-table with a cloth on top in a section of the store, have my own cash register on it and put slat wall behind me to hold up inventory? Man, what if I made flyers and passed them out to people outside of the store to attract them to the store to buy my products. I was thinking big, so big, I wonder if it would actually happen, but before that, I need to receive the box, the box with my inventory.

Few days after placing the order, after school, approximately at 2:45 pm, I get a phone call on my white Samsung flip phone, It's my mom!

Me: Hello.

Mom: Hey Dee? (Dee is my nickname that my mom gave me)

Me: Yeah

Mom: The box you've been waiting for came in today.

Me: Are you serious? I'm on my way.

Mom: Okay, see you soon.

The Box Arrived

As I am walking on the sidewalk of this busy road, walking to the store, I skip with glee passing two intersections. I am pumped up and excited. The moment I've been waiting for has arrived, the box was at the store waiting for me. A ten-year-old with a business, that is not something you hear every day. I arrived at the store, walked to the back of the store and walked right up to the box, looking at the box with a growing smile on my face and a glare in my eyes.

The box I've been waiting for is right in front of me. I grabbed a pair of scissors and slid the tip of the scissor along the piece of tape slowly, being careful to not damage the box or the precious items inside. The feeling of excitement running through my blood, breathing slowly as the tape separates.

As soon as the box opened, I saw a clear plastic bag that held all the toys, I tore that box open from the top.

My mom started as an indirect influencer, by not necessarily telling me what to do, but by being around her, it triggered my curiosity as to how I can make money; my mom then became a verbal director when she gave me advice as to how I could start making money.

Andy's Kid Shop did not make a dollar, but it was a start of me understanding business. G & B Uniforms and Dental Shop generated an average foot traffic of two to four people every open day. Not every person that walked in had a child with him or her. Out of the two to four people that walked in on average per day, two children walked in with their parents per week.

Ignorantly, the probability of me making money working at Andy's Kid Shop was very slim! The foot traffic was just not there and there were not enough kids walking in. Here I go again, I had to figure out a way to make money, there is no way I can just be broke. Although the kids in my class were job-less and their only source of income was their weekly allowance, I had no choice. My parents didn't give me an allowance.

I recall one time where I did ask my dad for an allowance and he thought about it, and he laughed. He must have thought about the allowance he received at my age when he was in Haiti, which was nothing. However, do know, my parents did give me what I needed. They took care of their son's necessities with shelter, food and water. As a child, they did think of me and buy smaller toys and such but I always wanted what my friends had, the latest gadget, the latest cell phone and the newest clothe. They would sometimes say no to me and that irritated me.

As a toddler, if I hurt myself or after being physically disciplined, my parents would allow me to keep crying. Sometimes they would mimic my crying to my face showing that it had no effect on them. Experiencing that, I did not go to my parents and complain about not having money or complain about not getting what I asked for. Their facial response would be "What are you going to do about it."

Lemonade Stand

Lying on my bed, frustrated, with not much to do but watch TV, I had to figure a way to make some money but now more importantly, have some importance with my life. It was not about the money, I was bored.

In the house, we had basic cable, and after school, the same shows played on the TV, and it usually was reruns. Outside of the house, the other kids that I hung out with didn't get out of school until hours after I was dismissed from school. My options were limited. As I lied on my bed, I had a thought-of-greatness; a lemonade stand could make me a few dollars. I decided to implement the idea and make it happen.

The start-up capital for this business venture was zero dollars. I went into the household fridge to see if we had lemonade, and we did. I took the lemonade carton that my mom bought for the house and placed it on the kitchen table. In my house, we have two floors.

The kitchen was on the top floor; I went to the basement and got a small bookshelf table without a backboard and used it as the stand for the lemonade stand. I brought the bookshelf table outside, and placed it in front of my house at the edge of the sidewalk. I went back inside and got the lemonade, on my way out, I grabbed plastic cups from the pantry and set up shop outside of my house.

My house was on a cul de sac and there was not too much traffic, only local traffic passed through. I waited for hours and no one passed by but a few cars, and the drivers turned their heads, looked at me and then turned their heads back facing the road and kept going to their destination. I would have enjoyed watching reruns on TV better than doing the lemonade stand.

As I was about to close the lemonade stand and bring everything inside, one of my neighbors saw what I was doing and walked up to me and asked me "What are you doing?" I let her know I was running a lemonade stand and she can buy a cup of lemonade for a dollar. She supported me and bought one cup. That's all that was sold. It didn't work too well; I made one sale and drank lemonade from my own supply.

The Hustle Continues

I still did not go to my parents and complain about not having money or complain about not getting what I asked for. Their response would have still been "What are you going to do about it." So, I had to figure what I was going to do about it. Fortunately for me in the circumstances of having a lack of finances, living in Rhode Island had its perks of leaves and snow falling.

Around this time was fall and when the season of fall starts, the leaves from the trees start to fall onto the ground. I looked around and I saw the leaves on the ground, yellow leaves, brown leaves, and green leaves everywhere! Leaves were on the ground, on my neighbor's cars, on my neighbor's houses, their doorsteps, everywhere!

At my middle school, there was a self-employed landscaper that was hired by my school, St. Leo the Great. He was a white-rugged around the edges looking man. He had a full-scruffy beard; about 5 foot 9 inches tall, long brunette hair with a red hat, and was always dirty. He was personable; he would wave and say "hi" to me almost every time I saw him.

In my neighborhood, there were a lot of elderly residents that live with their spouse. Some of the residents allowed the leaves to settle in their yard and deteriorate by themselves, some residents did rake their own leaves, but one of the residents were not raking their own leaves, they hired the self-employed landscaper and he had a leaf blower and he'll move their leaves for them and of course they would pay him. I wanted in on that action, and make some money for myself.

To the right of my house, there was a small 100-square-foot shed where my dad kept a rake and other yard supplies. I took that rake and went door to door asking my neighbors if they wanted me to rake their yard. $10 a pop it would cost them for me to rake their yard. I started by going right across the street to my neighbor John's house.

(Knock-knock)

Me: "Hey John, I was wondering if you wanted me to rake your yard for you."

John: "Andy, no it's all set, I'll get to it later."

Me: "okay, thanks anyway"

Onto the next-door, walking and scratching my rake along the cement floor filled with rocks, and when the rake caught a rock, I would tug harder and make a spark. Finally reaching the next house and walking up to their door.

(Knock-knock)

Me: "Hey neighbor, I live not too far from you and I was

wondering if you wanted me to rake your yard for you."

Neighbor: "umm… how much are you charging."

Me: "only $10, I will do the front of the yard and bring all the leaves over there (pointing to the direction of the corner of the fence, where it would not be in the way of any passersby.)

Neighbor: "umm… not right now."

Me: "okay, thanks anyway"

The people that would ask me for my price but end up saying "no" would aggravate me because they were the neighbors that got my hopes up that they were going to hire me but then disappoint me when they turned me away. However, I came here to give a service in return for money, not to feel disappointed, onto the next door. Walking and scratching my rake along the cement floor filled with rocks, and when the rake caught a rock, I would tug harder and make a spark. Finally reaching the next house and walking up to their door.

(knock-knock)

Me: "Hey neighbor, I was wondering if you wanted me to rake your yard for you."

Neighbor: "well how much is it."

Me: "only $10, I will do the front of the yard and bring all the leaves over there (pointing to the direction of the corner of the fence, where it would not be in the way of any passersby.)

Neighbor: "sure, can you start now?"

Keep Going

I finally got a customer and just made $10 when I would have spent that time sitting down, watching TV. Onto the next door, and I would repeat this cycle of knocking on doors, trying to get raking jobs until it was dark outside. When it became dark outside, it was time for me to go home. I may end the day off with $20 dollars in my pocket, or maybe $50 in my pocket.

When it got dark outside and I would go home. The next day, after school ended, I would repeat the cycle all over again going to different houses. My immediate neighborhood had one inlet from the main street and was in the shape of a large rectangle with houses throughout the perimeter of the rectangle and houses that cut through the rectangle on four different streets that were parallel to each other. I knocked on every door in my immediate neighborhood, and it was time for me to go outside of my neighborhood, but I didn't want to do it alone.

An entrepreneur once said something along the lines of "it is better to own 70% of $1,000,000 than own 100% of $100,000." Meaning bringing on help and growing a company exponentially is more profitable than doing it yourself when the income is substantially lower without the help.

I told my sixth-grade classmate, Leo what I was doing and how I was making money, and I asked him for help; the number of doors that I had to go through was so high that if I had help, I could potentially reach more doors. Leo wanted to work with me. Coincidentally, Leo was also my neighbor that lived in my immediate neighborhood. Leo's dad had a rake in his garage and Leo took that rake and came along side me of this business of raking leaves. All the money we would make, we would split; 50% would go to Leo and 50% would go to me.

After school, we went home, put our bags down, eat food and met up at the park that was in the middle of our neighborhood and start going to different houses outside of the neighborhood to rake. One door, two doors, three doors, four... Some would say no, some would say yes, some would say, "come back later", regardless, we were working!

Some days, we traveled miles outside of our neighborhood and on one of those days a lady driving by a house we were raking, asked us how much do we charge to rake, and we said "$10 for the yard." She said okay, how about I give you $50 to rake my yard. Leo and I looked at each other in awe and said yeah! We exchanged numbers, she gave us her address and she set an appointment for us to rake her yard.

She lived in the nicer part of the state, Cumberland, RI. When the day arrived, Leo's dad drove us to the house in Cumberland. Leo and I got dropped off and we walked up to the front door and "ding-dong-dong," I rang the doorbell. Here came this lady in her 40s to the door and said "Welcome guys." She directed us to the yard and had a leaf blower ready for us to use.

Her yard was bigger than any of the yards we worked on in Pawtucket. We now understood why she wanted to pay us $50. We were used to using only rakes but the leaf blower was more efficient. Leo and I alternatively used the leaf blower, while I raked; Leo blew the leaves into one big pile, and I organized his mess and after a few moments, we switched. I blew the leaves into one big pile, and Leo organized my mess until the entire yard was clean with two piles of leaves in one corner. The lady had brown-paper yard bags that we used to discard the leaves, the yard was spotless; we did it, another happy customer!

The winter quickly crept up on us during our business venture, we continued the yard cleaning business through the winter, but instead of using rakes, we used shovels. It was the same process, go door-to-door, and pitch our services and work for the doors that said "yes."

5

IMPLEMENT YOUR IDEAS

"All your ideas may be solid or even good, but you have to Actually EXECUTE on them for them to matter."
                                        –Gary Vaynerchuck

How many times have you thought of something that was good; said it was a good idea and did nothing about it? Ideas are thoughts, and thoughts can be things. This is based on the principle that the ideas and thoughts you have in your head can become tangible things when backed by action of implementation. The next step from having a successful idea is implementation, but this is rarely done.

Oxford dictionary defines **Implementation** as "The process of putting a decision or plan into effect." In short, implementation is just making it happen, the process of taking an idea and turning it into reality.

Ideas Are Not Accidental

Imagine Facebook still being in Mark Zuckerberg's mind and only in his mind, as if there was no Facebook.com, what would the online communication between family members and friends look like? The reason you can visit Facebook.com today is because Mark and his team took an idea, figured out how to create and market the platform. Some of your ideas that are implemented usually have an effect that is bigger than you and it affects other people.

My personal use of Facebook has begun relationships for me that would have changed the course of my life without it. For others, there are individuals that they met their now significant other on Facebook, got married and started a family.

This means there are children alive today that would have not been alive if it was not for Mark Zuckerberg actualizing his thoughts-of-greatness into reality. However, exactly what Facebook is today has been reported to not have been exactly what Mark envisioned in his mind before the creation of Facebook. However, with him actualizing his thoughts-of-greatness, which is simply directions, it allowed him to create what Facebook is today.

Great ideas do not come to you in the form of a thought-of-greatness for no reason or by accident. Great ideas are given to you in the form of a thought to make into reality because God knows your capabilities, weaknesses and strengths and chose you to carry out that idea and actualize that thought-of-greatness. You've been chosen to do spectacular things in your life, not live a life of mediocrity and averageness.

The implementation stage is crucial because this stage is the beginning of either a **blessing** or a **lesson**. For this chapter, the blessing is having created something unique and spectacular that the world can benefit from or the blessing is the attainment of a yearning of something, such as money. The lesson would typically mean the implementation of a thought-of-greatness, or idea that would ultimately end in failure but throughout the implementation phase; there would be many key points that would be learned and can be used for future ventures.

Before your blessing there are usually many lessons that teach you how to attain and maintain your blessing. **Many people want their blessing before putting forth any work that is required to receive it.** To maintain your blessing, you must learn by a series of events that has consciously or has unconsciously taught you the rules of attainment and maintenance.

There are a small group of individuals that received a large blessing but were not able to maintain it because it was received without the proper series of events that would allow the understanding of maintenance. In 1988, William "Bud" Post won the Pennsylvania Lottery, he won $16.2 Million dollars. Within nearly a year, he was $1 Million dollars in debt. It has been reported William lives on food stamps. In the case of Evelyn Adams, she won the lottery twice, once in 1985 and again in 1986, but reported by AskMen.com, she gambled it away and lives in a trailer park.

When working towards a goal, and in being successful, you become an individual with the mindset that can attain and maintain the blessing. I repeat, when working towards a goal, and in being successful, you become an individual with the mindset that can attain and maintain the blessing.

Attain and Maintain the Blessing

Without going into detail of his story, the "Gangsta" rapper, Curtis "50 Cent" Jackson is an epitome of working towards a goal, being successful, and becoming an individual with the mindset that can attain and maintain the blessings. He was raised in the gritty neighborhood of South Jamaica, Queens, NY. In 1994, 50 Cent was arrested for selling vials of cocaine to an undercover officer. Three weeks later, 50 Cent was arrested when police searched his home and found drugs. He was later sentenced to three to nine years in prison but he only served six months.

He began selling drugs at twelve years old and in the drug game you must have a *take it to make it* mentality and a *kill or be killed* mentality. Like a soldier in combat with an enemy, you must kill or be killed. Curtis uses that mentality in his businesses and music career which is part of the reason he is successful and is able to attain his blessings.

Curtis wasn't given the blessings he has due to his talent; he received the blessings due to him being chosen, implementing his thoughts-of-greatness, and using previous life-learned lessons from the drug game to attain the blessings. During his music career, in addition to his losses, 50 Cent cultivated a work ethic that could achieve its monetary equivalence, and doing this allowed him to maintain his blessings.

In 50 Cent's case, he received those lessons from uncontrollable situations as he was raised in an environment which was surrounded with drugs and drug dealing. Not only can lessons be taught by uncontrollable situations but lessons can come in the form of poor business decisions, unforeseeable circumstances, deprived conditions, and negative events.

Opening Andy's Kid Shop was a lesson. I did not make any money, but I did learn the basic understanding that a business' objective is to be profitable and how profit is made. It did come as a financial cost to my mom's pocket that 10 years later the inventory that was purchased is still in my shed in the same box that I was impatiently waiting for.

What If Syndrome

Have you ever asked yourself What If? For example, when you are out and about and an attractive man or a women is in your presence and you think to yourself, should I start a conversation with him or her, or not. You contemplate this for many moments. Going through your mind is the pros of starting a conversation. You think about the new relationship that can start because of your action of walking up to him or her and saying Hi. Thoughts about possible dates run through your mind, with you and that person together, walking, talking and smiling. What negates those positive thoughts are negative thoughts that lead you to not start that conversation.

While you were internally imbalanced, you succumbed to the negative thoughts and you did not start that conversation. While you were going back and forth from thinking about starting that conversation, he or she walked away and you missed your opportunity. Days passed by and you asked yourself, What If? What if I did talk to him or her and that conversation started a relationship that resulted in a family? What if that conversation helped you advance in your career because that individual knew someone that you did not know? Because you did not act, you are only stuck with what if.

This "what if" eventually could become an "I wish." This is dependent on the importance of the scenario. If it is about a woman or man that you missed an opportunity to speak to, you will very likely forget about him or her. However, if it is about your thoughts-of-greatness, that "what if" eventually could become an "I wish."

Imagine your thoughts-of-greatness, your dreams, your goals, your aspirations; If you do not act on them, what would that self-talk on your deathbed look like? In most cases, as you look back, the self-talk would start with "I wish…" (Then make a statement about what you wish you did versus what you actually did)

Spend some time with elderly individuals that are in a nursing care or hospice. You will find that their thoughts-of-greatness are dying with them and nothing can be done. You will also find their deepest regrets was not attempting to actualize their thoughts-of-greatness and that elderly individual wishes they could. Keep in mind on the word attempting, their deepest regrets were not *attempting* to actualize their thoughts-of-greatness, not necessarily actualizing their thoughts-of-greatness. It is one thing to make your thought-of-greatness come true, it is another to try. If at minimum you do not try, when you get older, you could get stuck with **What If Syndrome** and it could eventually become **I Wish Syndrome**.

Are you currently holding yourself back from doing something, that in the future, when you are elderly and on your deathbed, you will regret not acting?

Eric Thomas, a motivational speaker once said "take advantage of the opportunity of a lifetime, in the lifetime of the opportunity."

Listen to me… **Take Action!**

Message: For a moment, stop reading here and reflect on the last three paragraphs in this chapter. Reread if you must.

6

THE REAL YOU

"When you want something out of life, you've got to be willing to go into action, don't wait around for things to be just right, don't wait for things to be perfect, don't wait for the ideal situation, it will never be ideal."

–Les Brown

I believe the crusty floor was due to the drying of the tiled floor after cleaning it with the wrong chemicals by the previous tenant. I'm lying down on the black crusty floor, my head is against the door, to my left is a white ceramic sink, to my right a dusty white painted wall and my feet are running against the toilet. I am grabbing my head while I'm thinking about what I am going to do.

I'm in such disarray and I don't even know how I allowed myself to get into this position. I am sad and in so much mental pain but what is going on with me? I am in this tight bathroom, in complete darkness, tears running down my face, thinking of what I did, and now thoughts are running through my mind of what I need to do. From when I was shoveling snow and leaves, nine years had passed. I am now the owner of Progression Wireless, a wireless telecommunication sales company. In layman's term, we sold cell phones. I am sure you would like to know how I got here.

How It All Started

After I graduated high school, I had a thought-of-greatness that my life had meaning greater than being just an employee. I had a desire to go into business for myself, but I had no idea what to do, or where to start. I spoke with my previous employer about it, but every response he gave me was indirectly influencing me to start a business, that he was involved in, which was for his benefit and not necessarily mine. However, the desire that I had to open my own business was strong.

My then job was a general manager at a cell phone store, my friend and then co-worker, Jorge and I were working out late-at-night at the fitness center. As we were leaving the gym, walking to our cars, Jorge was walking on my right; Something came across his mind to tell me that he believed in me and he suggested that I go into business for myself, and he would quit the company we both worked for at the time, and embark on this journey with me in starting a business. He verbally gave me directions and suggested we open a cell phone store. This is what I needed, this was the direction that I was looking for to start my thoughts-of-greatness.

My thoughts-of-greatness and goals were already along the lines of me running my own business. Although I was running a cell phone store as an employee, I had no idea of what type of business I would open. Jorge's verbal direction for me to open a cell phone store was aligned with my thoughts-of-greatness and therefore I moved forward with it. We both had the experience of wireless telecommunication sales and within two months, Jorge and I sent our three-week intent to leave notice to our employer; there was no turning back now. Three weeks later, we started Progression Wireless in June 2014.

We started with one cart in one of the local malls in my area. My company expanded; I went from owning one store to two, then three, then four.

Store #1 North Attleboro, MA — August 18, 2014

The people who started the company went from Jorge and I to adding an employee, to adding another employee, to others. I am not going to tell you that operating the business was a breeze and it was easy because it was not. There were many long nights and early mornings. There were a lot of sacrifices that were made, but Progression Wireless became a business generating thousands upon thousands of dollars.

The Goal for the Company

My thoughts-of-greatness at the time included Progression Wireless becoming a national company, with hundreds of locations nationwide. This is what Jorge and I and the rest of the Progression Wireless team discussed. With every store we opened, our expansion plan had an unspecified end goal of hundreds of stores. I was self-aware and knew I was different than my peers in my environment. My middle school teacher did pull me aside and tell me this. I was different in the regards of what I wanted out of life and how I wanted to live my life.

In high school the feeling of not being average was growing stronger; I started listening to motivational speakers, and embodying their teachings. From that point on, I started believing that anything I can think of in my mind is possible and I shall live without limits. This was difficult because I was imbalanced with one side of me being pulled in one direction by indirect influencers and verbal directors in my ear, and additionally my limiting belies were holding me back, and on the other side, my thoughts-of-greatness that were supported by the motivational speakers that I listened to.

I wanted to share this mindset of actualizing thoughts-of-greatness with people who were around me. When you have a good feeling, or a great experience with something, it is natural to want to share to allow someone else to experience it.

My mind was so open and my idea of greatness was getting so big that it felt good and I wanted other people to experience that. I was going through a time of personal development and I was hoping other people would be interested in doing the same thing. Happiness comes from progressing daily and since I wanted to create a culture of people progressing, therefore I called the company Progression Wireless. The idea I had was that for each employee of Progression Wireless, I will instill the mindset of progression and create individuals that were going after their goals.

Progression Wireless would become a filter for many individuals from all walks of life from below average people to people that knew their thoughts-of-greatness. I hoped each employee would learn a skill set or understand their vision for their life and they would pursue it rather than be average. My ultimate goal was to change the mindset of individuals throughout the world from within my company. This goal was far-fetched however I believed in it and that is why I pursued it, until my employee, Joe told me something that changed the course of my life and the company's future.

My motivation for growing the company started getting weaker and weaker by the day. I went from working every day to working once to two times a week and delegating all my responsibilities to my employees. Many would say that I was "living the life of a boss," where I get paid and don't have to work too much. However, it did not help in our expansion plan or in my goal to change the world. Therefore, I was feeling unfulfilled. I started waking up not wanting to go to work; in my own company! The people that kept me going was Joe and Jorge as they were constantly reminding me of the reason the company even started, change the world through our expansion plan.

Is this just a job?

From the point the company began I started to instill the principles I learned through motivational speakers into my employees. I wanted to teach my employees to be the best version of themselves, and doing that forced me to continually work on myself to be a role model for each employee. For each employee, I took time out of the day to talk about their personal goals and values, I let him or her know my goal in this company is to progress every single person.

It wouldn't be long until Jorge shed light that to some employees, Progression Wireless was just a job and they weren't interested in progressing, they were fine with being complacent. I was in disbelief, until months passed and I became consciously aware that what Jorge said was true, and I was heartbroken. I would look in the mirror and question: in my employee's lives, is all my hard work going to waste? Am I growing a company for pure profit? I worked so much harder when I believed that my work was going towards the betterment of the lives of my employees and their families.

Andy & Jorge at Store #3
Providence, RI – August 2015

After Jorge let me know that many individuals were simply working for a paycheck and not interested in progressing, I immediately halted the speed of the company's expansion and audited the people that were working for me. I knew the only way this company would grow at the speed I wanted to grow it at, everyone would have to be interested with progressing their personal lives. I understood that you can get the best work from an employee only if they are truly progressing with their personal goals, meaning they are truly happy and not putting on a fake smile for work.

While auditing the employees, I had to figure each employee's true intention while working for me. I had to figure out what value can each employee add to the team; as the team is only as strong as its weakest link.

The only way I could've grown the company to the size that I wanted, the only way I could've impacted the world the way I wanted to, and the only way I could affect each team member is by not having a weak link. Although Jorge told me that some employees were simply working to get paid and could not care any less about becoming a better person, and I saw the truth in that, I had to figure out for myself why was that, why is it that someone could possibly not care about their future and their dreams.

I could not fathom someone going through the flow of life and they took whatever life threw at them versus working towards a goal. Jorge was right, but I just had to figure out why some were complacent and get them to realize that they are great individuals and the real version of themselves had to be released.

Your Two Versions

There are two versions of you, the real version of you, which is called, The Real You. The Real You is a version of you that is living out your thoughts-of-greatness. And the other version of you is a version of you that is not living your thoughts-of-greatness or not making your thoughts-of-greatness a reality, this unfortunate version of yourself is The Unfulfilled You.

For a visual representation, I locate The Real You as a small human being in the middle of your chest that is living dormant. And I locate The Unfulfilled You as the outer being of your body. Making your thoughts-of-greatness a reality is bringing The Real You to life and expanding that small human being in the middle of your chest to filling your entire body.

Day after day, I focused less on profitably and more on The Real You training in each employee. Since it was illegal to have someone be at work and not pay him or her for their time, I invested time and money into their paychecks without them necessarily bringing in profit to the company.

Some employees I had were not an asset to the company but my belief in their progression and them becoming the person that was in their chest would be worth it in the long run. A culture of personal progression was being built. Some corporate presidents and chief executive officers would disagree with my tactic on the company culture. They thought the company culture I was building would be the recipe of a failed business, but I put People over Profit. Putting people over profit was found to be advantageous to my company.

What I learned was that the company culture I was

building would be only be beneficial to 20% of my employees. These employees came into the company without drive or hustle and within months, they were not only focus on Progression Wireless, but would also focus and work on their personal progression.

This built loyal employees, and employees that were driven to make Progression Wireless a growing company. Although 20% of the employees were following the mindset of progressing and working on their thoughts-of-greatness and becoming the real version of themselves, there was a remaining 80% that were not following the mindset of progressing and working on their thoughts-of-greatness and becoming the real version of themselves. My focus quickly turned to the 80% that was not doing that. If each employee was not 100% focused on releasing the best version of themselves, I recognized that made me a failure.

I then spent more time with each employee, I brought them out to dinner, and talked to him or her about their personal lives to try to figure out what can be done to show them their greatness and living a life of mediocrity is not for them. I spent time studying the basics of the mind, the basics of entrepreneurship and why so many people live unfulfilled lives and how to change the mindset. I listened to motivational speakers; in the workplace, in hopes that it would enter the **subconscious mind** of the employees that were listening, I had the speeches of motivational speakers playing in the background.

After doing this for so long, I was exhausted with trying to change people and showing them their greatness. The leaders in my company, which were Jorge, the inventory manager; Joe, the manager of all stores; Jarixa, the office manager and myself, the business owner, we held weekly meetings. In one of those meetings, I expressed the exhaustion I had with what I was doing and held my head low while trying to figure out what my next step would be.

Joe saw the frustration in my face with my failed attempts and he said something that would change the way I trained and even changed the way I thought about interacting with people.

Joe turned to me and said "Andy, you cannot *change* someone, you can only help people help themselves." The simplest words, with the simplest meaning allowed me to see something that I had not seen before. The simplest words, with the simplest meaning showed me where I was going wrong this entire time as far as trying to change people.

Joe & Andy Before a Company Meeting — September 2015

What I understood before Joe told me this was if I could show the people that I could actualize my thoughts-of-greatness, then they will envision greatness for themselves; act on it and be able to do it as well. I showed the 80% of my employees that was not fulfilling the real version of themselves, that their goals and dreams are possible.

However, where I went wrong was I was basing it off my dreams, my values, my goals and what my beliefs were. Not only that, what I also learned was that 80% of my employees were comfortable with where they were at in their lives and nothing I can do can change them. And it was at that point I realized what I was doing, I was trying to change people into something that they were not and get them to believe in something that they did not believe.

Termination of a Weak Link

Progression Wireless Store #3 (pictured on pg. 58) was a 48 square-foot cart in the mall's food court area. The cart had a flat surface with cell phone displays on both sides. One end of the cart was the store's computer, cash register and point-of-sale system. In front of that system was the chair the employees could sit on while completing a transaction.

A method we used to attract potential customers to the store and purchase was cold-greeting. Cold-greeting is when a potential customer walks by the store, the employee would greet them without having any prior relationship, attempt to find information about their current cell phone and persuade the customer as to why our cell phones were beneficial to them.

One day I went to the store unannounced and from a distance, I saw a female Progression Wireless employee, Crystal, sitting down using her phone, when her job was to greet potential customers as they walked by the cart. I looked at the cart for a period of time watching to see if she was performing her duties or not. She was not performing her duties.

I approached the cart and started a conversation with Crystal. I then brought her to a table in the food court and had a one-on-one conversation with her. I explained the company's policy with greeting, the reason for it and what it can do for her paycheck, as each employee received a commission for each cell phone sold. She then explained to me that her hourly pay is suffice and she did not need more money. In her mind, she believed that based on her weekly base pay, she was getting "money."

I told her about larger amounts of money that was possible for her to make, if she did the work, she declined and continued to express her paycheck was suffice. This average thinking was a cancer, and I felt I could change her mind in due time, until I remembered what Joe told me, "Andy, you cannot *change* someone, you can only help people help themselves."

I terminated Crystal on sight and took all company property within her possession. She was one of the weakest links in my company. With her complacent attitude, she was a bad apple, which would affect the rest of the employees therefore causing harm to the company culture I built and furthermore; if she could not see a better future for herself, there is nothing I could do for her. This got me thinking…

I recall an incident with Joe that was very similar of him not greeting; after explaining the reason for greeting and the progression he could make personally and the additional money he could make in his paycheck; Joe asked me to teach him how to greet. The difference between Crystal and Joe was that Joe was part of the 20% and Crystal was part of the 80%.

Joe was teachable, he wanted to make more money, he wanted to progress, he wanted me to teach him how to. Crystal was okay with her circumstances and couldn't care less if I taught her or not. I then learned that all my hard work with the Crystal was going in one ear and out the other. Joe wanted to improve, I helped him in doing so. Crystal did not want to improve, therefore there is nothing that can be done to help her progress. *I can only help people help themselves.*

Wake Up the Real Me

I headquartered the office a few miles from that mall. In the office, there were desks and shelves where the inventory was kept. I sometimes worked at night in the office alone. On a particular night, I was working in the office by myself. While I was there, I was getting frustrated with the company's finances and I was getting frustrated with the 80% not caring about progressing. Across from the desk from where I was working, was the bathroom with the black crusty floor.

I ran in there during an emotional breakdown, laid down and put my head against the door, touched the white ceramic sink that was on my left, and had my right arm on the dusty white painted wall and had my feet running against the toilet.

I am grabbing my head while I'm thinking about what I am going to do. I'm in such disarray and I don't even know how I allowed myself to get into this position of lack of finances. I am in so much mental pain at the time but what was going on with me. I lock myself in this tight bathroom in complete darkness, tears running down my face, thinking of what I did, and now thoughts are running through my mind of what I need to do. Little did I know The Real Me was going to speak to me that night.

I left the office and walked to the silver four door sedan that I was driving, and in the darkness of the night, sat in the car and I prayed to God. I prayed he remove me from the situation I was in, with the fact that I was not wanting to work at Progression Wireless anymore, with the fact I was responsible for the paycheck of all my employees and there was a lack of finances, for the fact that I was failing at building a culture of 100% of my employees wanting to progress and because I was not truly living out the real version of myself. I felt like a failure; I was a leader of a company that was focused on progressing and 80% of my employees were complacent.

As I sat in the car, I was reminded of what Joe told me, "You cannot *change* someone, you can only help people help themselves." You determine where it is that you want to go, you determine if you will be open-minded enough to accept help from another person. You are truly responsible for your destiny and no one can do anything for you. You determine The Real You. I had to help myself and determine the real version of myself and make a change.

I left the office, and drove home. I arrived home and went straight to my bedroom, turned on the music streaming application, Pandora Internet Radio, lied on my bed with my face down and a song played that would then change everything as I knew.

The song started with "Once I was seven years old..." The song's lyrics told the story of a young man. In lyrical form, this young man sang about when he was once seven years old and the things he had done at that age. I was able resonate with him and think back to when I was seven years old and recall the things I used to do. He then went on to sing about his life at eleven years old, which I also resonated with his eleven-year-old self as I thought back to my pre-teen days.

He swiftly went from singing about his eleven-year-old self to singing about his twenty-year-old self, and I resonated with that since I was twenty-years-old at the time, then he was singing about his future thirty and sixty-year-old self. He made a comment that his dad only received sixty-one years, and that is when I looked up from my bed and saw that I had to live the life that was in my chest, The Real Me.

The singer sang about him going from adolescent years to elderly years, in less than four-minutes. I realized life was too fast, I knew if I did not make a decision to live my life as The Real Me, I'd be doing myself an injustice. I had a successful business, friends, money, and family but I wasn't happy. To figure out what I truly wanted, what The Real Me truly wanted, I had to figure out the values that I wanted to live my life by and define them.

7

ALL IN OR NOTHING

Before you are aware about what you must do to become who you must be, commit to yourself. If you have mentally woken up and are ready to live your life as the real version of yourself, sign by the lowercase **x** below.

Today marks the day you will be moving forward with making your thoughts-of-greatness a reality.

Making your thoughts-of-greatness a reality may be the most difficult mission you will ever take on in your life; this mission effects many people, including yourself. Making your thoughts-of-greatness a reality will take total commitment to truly living the best version of yourself.

You must be committed and make a promise to yourself but also to the people your thoughts-of-greatness effect. Here, you must be honest with yourself.

x_____

Date: _____

Message: As you continue to read, It is suggested you take notes and use a highlighter to highlight the topics you connect with.

Let Your Friends Know of Your Mindset

<u>Highlight</u> Your Favorite Part. Take a Photo of It.

Post the Photo on Twitter, Facebook or Instagram
#NoMoreAverage   **@CantQuitAndy**

8

VALUES OF TOIL

"It's not hard to make decisions when you know what your values are."

–Roy E. Disney

Even though the feeling of dissatisfaction of my everyday life quickly swept over me right after the night I laid with my face down in my bed listening to the song about the seven year old: "Once I was seven years old..." on Pandora Internet Radio, it was imperative that I go to work and continue to lead the company that I had built. However, on a daily basis, it consumed my mind that I was not, but should be actualizing my thoughts-of-greatness.

I ran a cell phone business, but I felt disconnected from my thoughts-of-greatness and my thoughts-of-greatness were calling me every day. Even as the owner of my company, I started to dread the five business days, which made up 71% of my life. I had to do something about it, I just did not have the answer of what to do next.

Although Joe did not usually work from the company office, where the company was headquartered; one day I was in the office working with him. Joe was working at one of the desks and I was working at another. At random I asked Joe what his values of toil were.

He had no clue what I was talking about. I left my desk, walked over to his desk, kneeled down as he was sitting down with his chair facing my direction and I broke it down for him. **Values of toil** is a list of fundamental principles or standards that you set for the work you will perform and the description of the characteristics of the way you want to live your life, or live the next chapter in your life. **Toil** is the work you do, not what your job is, I am talking about where and what your efforts are being spent on or how you live your life.

I let him know the way to figure this out is to write down, in bullet points, the way you want your future efforts to be exhausted. After writing your values of toil list down, the list is to be examined and you will audit your current situation with the list. You then make adjustments to your current situation or create a strategy for your life to match the principles or standards of your values of toil. When making a strategy to match the principles or standards of your values of toil, this is considered a life goal. Joe and I wrote down our values of toil, a few that I wrote down were

- My work will allow me to travel from state to state
- I will not be grounded to one area due to inventory or employees
- My work will be mobile from a laptop, and I could technically work on a beach
- I will be aiding in the progression of other individuals
- Mentors will be able to pour into me to aid in my

success

- I am the owner of the company I work for
- I can maximize revenue from one location versus multiple locations

These values came from what I wanted to be doing based on my prior work history. My first value came because I was used to working in one state, and I wanted to be able to travel and have business done interstate. My second value was written because Progression Wireless' business structure was a stationary storefront, which included training and maintaining employees and keeping inventory in one location, which did not support my first value.

My third value was my first value reiterated and clearly defined. My fourth value was written because of my experiences at Progression Wireless, I would be focused on helping people help themselves in their progression, rather than trying to change them. My fifth value was written because I understood there were people who had more experience in a certain field than I did, I wanted to make sure that I put myself in a position that I can be around people that I wanted to emulate.

My sixth value was written because I wanted to make sure I was in total control of the hours that I worked, the money I made, and used my creativeness to create a business that would generate revenue and that the assets could be left to my future kids. My seventh value was written because I wanted to position my company in a way that I could generate revenue from one location rather than multiple locations.

Listed were just seven values from my full page of my values of toil and then I realized Progression Wireless did not match it entirely. Although it was a hard decision and I would end up feeling that my hard work would go to waste, at that point of writing my values of toil, I decided to make a plan to close Progression Wireless and live the thoughts-of-greatness that would be aligned with my values of toil. I just did not where I would go to next.

Without a clear understanding of your values of toil, the life goals you set for your life's work will be much harder to define. Your values of toil list are to be used to determine if an opportunity, such as a job, lifestyle or etc., matches your values and not a short-term pleasing.

Although I was making decent money owning Progression Wireless, a clear value of my toil is "I will not be grounded to one area due to inventory." All the inventory, which were the cell phones, were placed at the stores, but I felt The Real Me wanting to travel for work and meet people from different walks of life and that lived throughout the world.

Progression Wireless was not large enough to operate without me for an extended period of time. Therefore, this aspect of Progression Wireless was not aligned with the values of where and what my efforts were being spent on. The short pleasing would be me operating Progression Wireless because it was the easy way out. The hard way out would be closing Progression Wireless and figuring out what I wanted to do based on my values of toil.

When you clearly define your values, use this as that checklist to determine if an opportunity is right for you or not, based on your values. There are individuals that their values are not clear and they take whatever is given to them (ride the current instead of paddle the water.) Refer to Chapter 3, Pg 31.

9

GOAL SETTING

"A dream written down with a date becomes a GOAL. A Goal broken down into steps becomes a PLAN. A Plan backed by ACTION makes your dreams come true."

–Greg Reid

Writing your goal(s) down is telling your subconscious mind what it is you would like it to attain for you. We will go into an example. Jeff is the co-owner of JB's Moving Services, and he and his partner, Justin is in the business of furniture moving and delivery. He helps furniture companies by delivering their inventory to their customers.

In addition to that, he also helps people throughout the country move from one house to another house. He is starting this business and his goal for the business is to get a truck. He searches online "how to set goals."

He learns that he must define his goals, and where he learns how to define a goal was not as clear as it is in this book. On his goal sheet, he writes down "Buy a truck for the business by January 1." By writing this down he has asked his subconscious mind to buy a truck for the business by January 1.

This is exactly what his subconscious mind is working on. Now his subconscious mind continually presents all sorts of trucks to Jeff's attention. One truck is a Ford-F150, but this is not what Jeff needs and he is frustrated that he can't find what he wants.

A Goal is a defined objective you are trying to achieve through your efforts within a fixed time frame. The basics of goal setting begin with a pen and a pad. To increase the probability of your goal(s) being achieved, you must write your goal(s) down and follow the rules below for setting goals.

Writing down your goal(s) forces you to clearly identify what it is that you want, when you want it and why you want it. You live in your subconscious mind, and writing your goals down is your conscious mind writing a letter directly to your subconscious mind as to what it is you want it to do for you.

Your brain is not configured to memorize long paragraphs. It is much easier to memorize bullets points than it is to memorize long paragraphs. For the easy recall of your goals, the easy transmission of your goals to your subconscious mind and the remembrance of your reasoning, it is imperative to write down each respective portion of your goal in response to each step as its own bullet point. Here are the steps to goal setting.

1.   **Define the end result.** In one to three sentences, specifically write down the end result of your goal. What will your goal look like when you have achieved

it? Be sure to include the dates, and exact particulars, as this needs to be detailed. In this part, be sure to write the sentence(s) in the present tense. Write that the only reason this goal was achieved was because steps 2 through 12 were executed in the time that you said you would execute the steps.

2. **Write down the goal** you want to accomplish and the date you will accomplish it by, with your name in the first sentence. (Be specific in details, with numbers, and accurate/particular descriptions.)

3. **Acknowledge and complete your goal prerequisites.** Some goals require a task to be completed before the goal can be accomplished. Your prerequisite can be done before starting on this goal, or can be done simultaneously while working on accomplishing this goal (e.g. to buy a car, you may need to earn the money to buy it, while you are searching for the car to buy) (This step may not be applicable to every goal.)

4. **Write down the reason** you want to complete this goal; go into detail, explain your emotions behind this goal, and write down the people it may indirectly or directly positively effect.

5. **Write down incompletion affects.** Write down what will happen if you do not complete the goal. Writing down what will happen will tell your subconscious mind that there is no option and that it must be completed.

6. **Write down daily basis requirements.** This is what you will do daily to be sure this goal comes to pass.

7. **Write down who'll keep you accountable.** In achieving this goal, when you are being held accountable, the probability of you accomplishing your goal(s) increases to 85%. (This step may not be applicable to every goal.)

8.   **Write down who will be helping you** in the attainment of your goal (e.g. personal trainer for a weight-loss goal). (This step may not be applicable to every goal.)

9.   **Define your middle mark.** Your middle mark is defined as your halfway point towards your goal. Your goal may be so grand that it seems very difficult to reach. Identify and define the point that you are halfway towards completing your goal and make your plans to reach your halfway point. Once you reach your halfway point, then make a plan to complete your goal.

10.   **Write down ahead of time and acknowledge small wins.** Be sure to be aware of the small accomplishments you will make towards your goal. Each small accomplishment that is acknowledged is a reward to your subconscious mind and your subconscious mind will continue to want to be rewarded. Your subconscious mind will then work on accomplishing more small wins, getting closer to your goal daily. Before the completion of the goal, write down what each small win will be and acknowledge it when you reach it. (E.g. lost 2 lbs. of my 50 lbs. weight loss goal.)

11.   **Easy access.** Place your goal sheets in a place that you have easy access. Read your goal sheets daily, one time when you wake up, and in the middle of the day and right before you lay your head to rest. When the feeling of burnout, confusion, lack of motivation, or over exhaustion takes place, reread your goals.

12.   **Repeat your written goal.** Write down the goal you want to accomplish and the date you will accomplish it by, with your name in the first sentence. (Be specific in details, with numbers, and accurate/particular descriptions.)

Why would Jeff be frustrated? His subconscious mind is giving him exactly what he asked for. He wanted a truck. A Ford-F150 is an 8-foot truck. However, this 8-foot truck will not be beneficial to his business as this truck is too small and won't be able to carry all the furniture he needs to carry at any given time. What he needs is a 24-foot truck. This is what happens with your goals.

Your subconscious mind does what you tell it to do, but it may not give exactly what you want, unless requested, and it is because of how you define your goals. Instead of "Buy a truck for the business by January 1," This is how Jeff should have written down that goal:

- After executing all the things that I must do, will allow me to have in my possession, a standard-body new White Automatic 2018 Freightliner Business Class M2 truck before January 1 2018.

- I, Jeffery Barnes, will purchase a standard-body new White Automatic 2018 Freightliner Business Class M2 truck before January 1 2018.

- This vehicle will have a 24-foot body and it will be purchased for $83,495 including tax or less.

- The reason I want and need this truck is to be able to operate JB's Moving Services. Operating JB's Moving Services will put me in a position to provide for the house my wife, kids, and I live in and pay for food, water and other necessities that we need.

- If I do not complete this goal, I will not be able to run my business and my wife, kids and I will be homeless.

- To achieve this goal, I will search craigslist for two hours and visit a different truck dealership every Monday, Wednesday and Friday morning until I find the specific truck I am requesting.

●Justin will be helping me in finding this truck but I will not depend on him.

●Justin and I will meet every Saturday morning to discuss our search of finding the standard-body new White Automatic 2018 Freightliner Business Class M2 truck. My middle mark will be the completion of finding the truck.

●I must acknowledge each small win as each small win means I am getting closer to the completion of my goal. My small wins are as follows, a small win will be

      1) When I have been looking for the truck consistently for two weeks,

      2) When I have acquainted myself with six dealerships, letting them know I am in the market for a truck,

      3) When I find the truck that I want,

      4) When an offer is made on the desired truck.

●I, Jeffery Barnes, will purchase a standard-body new White Automatic 2018 Freightliner Business Class M2 truck before January 1, 2018.

Jeff is to repeat this goal out loud to himself every morning, every mid-day and every night before he rests his head on his bed. Usually your goals are written, but not specific and we take what life gives to us. Your subconscious mind is working to give you what you ask of it, nothing less, and nothing more. If you do not define the request, you will be dissatisfied with the results.

Awoken the Sleeping Giant

Before I opened the first store of Progression Wireless, I sat down in a quiet room, in a place where spiritual meditation usually takes place. In a calm state, I wanted to understand what The Real Me wanted to do and I clearly wrote down those goals, the reasoning and what I was willing to do to make it happen. I recall writing that I would open the first cell phone store in June and by quarter one of the following year, the second store would be in the works of opening.

This goal seemed nearly impossible as I had no idea what to expect in running a business, I just knew what I wanted to accomplish. What I did not know at the time, but do know now, was that my subconscious mind was working on making that goal a reality unbeknownst my conscious mind.

My subconscious mind was secretly strategizing how the second store would open and it would pass that message to my conscious mind at the right time and it did. My conscious mind received the message and shortly after, fear came over me. I was scared to expand, not knowing if I would be able to maintain two locations.

Instead of overcoming my fear, I became idle and did not decide to move forward with opening the second store just yet, until one day I was lying down in my bed with my eyes open and posed a question to myself, "If not now, when?" I had no answer for when, then I decided that it had to be now. I jumped out of my bed and decided to open the second location at that point. The sleeping giant has been awoken, once again.

Standing on the side of my bed, I put a song on by Ace Hood, called "Go N Get It." This song gave me the excitement and motivation for me to take the next step and search for the next location. Not only did I have to search for a location, I had to work much harder in increasing sales at the first store to have the capital to fund the opening of the next location. Within that small period of time I was able to do so, thanks to my goal setting and planning. It allowed me to have a clear direction as to where it is I wanted to go.

The subconscious mind works stronger than the conscious mind does and I overcame the fear that was in me. On December 22, nine-days before quarter one of the following year, I signed the lease for my second store. This is the power of writing goals down, as my goal of the second store being in the works of opening by quarter one of the subsequent year was achieved.

I am convinced school students, athletes, employees, sales persons, executive officers, managers, and individuals in charge of themselves or a team lose focus, drive and determination in their craft because of the lack of proper goal setting. The effect of incorrect goal setting is detrimental to success. It is even more detrimental to success as indirect influencers or verbal directors obscure the person's direction. When a goal is clearly defined, the person will realize everything that is aligned with their goal(s) and disregard anything that is not aligned with their goal(s).

Anything that is not aligned with your goal must be disregarded. What is not aligned with your goal distracts, or takes you off course from the completion of your goal. What is aligned with your goal will somehow help in the completion of your goal. By clearly telling your subconscious mind what it is that you want, everything aligned will fall in place by the directions of your subconscious mind to your conscious mind.

If your goals are not clearly defined, when indirect influencers or verbal directors sway you against your goals or thoughts-of-greatness, they can have you fall off track from your goals. But when your goals are clearly defined, when one of the two influencers attempt to influence you against your goals or thoughts-of-greatness, they'll have little to no power over your actions. Your subconscious mind will realize the request from them is not aligned with the goals you originally asked for it to achieve and your subconscious mind will disregard it.

In this example, Jonathan, the college's star point guard, his goal is to go to the NBA. He clearly defined his goal to be the starting point guard for the Los Angeles Lakers. For him to achieve this goal, he must physically be in the best shape he can be. Because he clearly understands the repercussion of him not achieving this goal; he must do everything that he can do in order to make sure his thoughts-of-greatness becomes a reality. It is proven that alcohol and marijuana can affect your body to not perform at its peak.

Therefore, when a verbal director invites Jonathan to smoke marijuana and drink alcohol, as many college students dibble-and-dabble into, he does not comply as it counteracts his thoughts-of-greatness and is not aligned with his goal.

Goal Vs. Fantasy

When goal setting, what many people tend to do is indulge in fantasy and confuse a fantasy with a goal. Oxford Dictionaries defines **Fantasy** as "the activity of imagining things, especially things that are impossible or improbable." A word that stands out to me is "improbable." Oxford Dictionaries defines Improbable as "not likely to be true or to happen." So, a fantasy is imaging things that are not likely to be true or not likely to happen. Forming a fantasy in place of a goal is a form of escapism. **Escapism** is defined as the tendency to search for distraction, amusement and relief from reality or routine. I know I just threw a bunch of definitions at you, but reread if you must.

During my freshmen year in high school, my third period class was math. In that math class was eighteen students, made up from a mixed variety of boys and girls that were Black, White, Cape-Verdean and Latino; I was the only Dark-Skinned Black student. In that class I met Patrick, we hit off our friendship rather quickly.

One thing Patrick and I had in common was our dislike for math as this third period math class was a special math course intended for students who do not do well in math. On a daily basis, Patrick and I spoke to each other in class versus do the math work. Right after third period was lunch in the downstairs cafeteria.

As we left the third period math class, everyday Patrick and I walked down the stairs to the cafeteria. As we walked into the cafeteria, we separated. Patrick and I sat at different lunch tables, because Patrick had his friends from his middle school that he sat with and I had my friends from my middle school that I sat with.

Patrick & Andy – Trip to Florida

As days went by in high school, my connection started getting stronger to Patrick and his lunch table group. I felt more connected with the individuals at Patrick's lunch table than the group that I sat with. The people that sat at Patrick's table were from Central Falls, so let's call them the "C.F. Kids." As the thought sat in my head for some time, one day right after getting my lunch meal from the cafeteria lady, I decided to go the C.F. Kids table and take a seat.

I fit right in, even though at the time I lived in Pawtucket, I fit in because I was originally from Central Falls. Part of the C.F. Kids was Devin. Patrick and Devin usually sat next to each other at the lunch table. Since Patrick and I were close because of the third period math class, it was natural for me to sit next to Patrick while sitting at this table of twelve people. Since Devin was hanging with Patrick, it was natural for me to hang with Devin as well. Devin, Patrick and I became a clique, we became best friends that eventually hung out during and after school.

When Devin and I hung out together, besides playing basketball, and checking out girls, Devin and I talked about our future. We spoke about what we wanted for ourselves in our near future. We spoke about owning businesses, traveling, cars we would have after we graduate high school and what we would be doing after graduation.

Devin wanted to be a Disc-jockey (DJ). Devin had a love for music and mixing it in a way a crowd could sing and dance to the songs. He was the life of the party, when we walked into a party together, within the moment he stepped into the event, all eyes turned on him, very personable he was; dapping up every guy in sight and giving kisses on the cheeks to the pretty ladies.

Devin had these high goals but I would later learn that it was never goals, they were fantasies. You see, Devin would talk and talk and talk about what life would be like when he is a professional DJ in the future; Devin would talk and talk and talk about the type of car he wants and his plan to move out of him mom's house. He had two types of faces that he would show when he spoke about his future. One of his facial expressions was a smirk on his lips with his left eye raised higher than his right eye whilst his eye balls were gazing into the sky as if he could visualize his future-self experiencing what he said would happen.

The other face was a serious facial expression where no facial muscle was used to show any expression besides his eyebrows that tensed up to show his seriousness; the words that came out of his mouth about his future, whatever he said with this face, the words were so strong and direct. Devin talked about his future self as if these were goals, but it was a high; it was a form of escapism to talk about what the future could be like because it allowed Devin to escape reality.

Devin spoke about saving money to purchase an Apple MacBook Pro for his DJ career that he was planning to have. He spoke about this Apple MacBook Pro for years and the years passed. Many times, Devin spoke about the DJ software, Serato; he *needed* to get Serato because the DJ software could do wonderful things for him as a DJ. With a smirk on his lips and his left eye raised higher than his right eye whilst his eye balls were gazing into the sky as if he could visualize himself getting an Apple MacBook Pro, "Andy, I'm going to get that MacBook Pro and I'll get Serato on it, watch" said Devin. Nearly a decade later, no Apple MacBook Pro, no Serato.

Devin is an average individual. His thoughts-of-greatness of being a DJ was being vicariously lived through other DJs that were actualizing their thoughts-of-greatness, and Devin tagged along. Understand it is very possible for Devin to get out of the average success group. Devin befriended a DJ that was living his thoughts-of-greatness and this DJ had a successful Event business where this individual traveled the country DJing events. Instead of Devin pursuing his own thoughts-of-greatness, Devin found it much easier to live vicariously through this DJ.

A **Goal** is a "defined objective you are trying to achieve through your efforts within a fixed time frame;" the key words are *trying to achieve through your efforts.* If you are not making any effort towards the objective within that fixed time frame, you are fantasizing; possibly fantasizing with the hope it may come true or fantasizing whilst knowing that it will not come true, but you enjoy the feeling of talking about it.

When you look at your goals, cross-out/disregard any goals that are not a commitment for you to bring to fruition. If you have not committed to the completion of a goal in the fixed time frame that you set, do not speak on this goal as you are simply indulging into fantasy.

10

THREE SUCCESS GROUPS

"There are three types of people in this world. Firstly, there are people who make things happen. Then there are people who watch things happen. Lastly, there are people who ask, what happened?"

–Steve Backley

From the experiences, study and research that I have done on human behavior and psychology; there are three different types of people: preeminent, average and subpar. Everyone belongs to one of the three success groups. The **preeminent success group** make up 2% of population, the **average success group** make up 95% of population and the **subpar success group** make up 3% of population. The group you are in, can have an effect, but do not dictate the amount of money you have, it is composed of three things: your thought process, your characteristics and your actions.

Success Groups
Preeminent (2%)
Average (95%)
Subpar (3%)

There is a small group of individuals that walk this planet that are either working on living their thoughts-of-greatness or have succeeded and are living their thoughts-of-greatness. The preeminent success group makes up about two percent of population.

An individual in the **preeminent success group** has a wealth of characteristics. This individual is a confident man or woman that is willing to accept responsibility for his or her actions. He or she has little to no limiting beliefs and is willing to do whatever it takes to live a fulfilled life.

He or she can lead by example and overcome all road blocks that appear in the way while attempting to accomplish his or her goals. This individual encourages other people to follow their thoughts-of-greatness. He or she accepts the unknown, and chooses to lead his or her life.

This individual works to live past his or her potential and he or she will accept responsibility for his or her current circumstance (good or bad). This individual can mentor and be a mentee, this individual is self-reliant, and has little to no excuses for failure. This individual is committed to actualizing his or her thoughts-of-greatness, he or she is optimistic and has accepted the responsibility to not be average.

The **average success group** makes up 95% of population. An individual in this group is living his or her life vicariously through, or is mimicking the qualities of other people. An individual in this group usually has thoughts-of-greatness but takes no responsibility in actualizing his or her thoughts-of-greatness and the people it affects, therefore this individual takes little to no action towards living those thoughts-of-greatness.

An individual in this group has the potential to be the best version of him or herself and to be successful if those thoughts-of-greatness are actualized, as actualizing those thoughts-of-greatness will lead him or her to success in due time.

However, with all this potential, he or she continues to remain idle, mimic others and not move forward in his or her favor. This individual may be aware of his or her goals and thinks about those goals often, but will not be committed to the achievement of said goals. The goals he or she is working towards may be goals that seem easy to attain, or is categorized as a fantasy.

The goals this individual may be working towards are goals set by indirect influencers and/or verbal directors, not goals aligned with his or her thoughts-of-greatness. This individual's closest friends will also be in the average success group or the subpar success group, affecting his or her chance to get out of the average success group. Jim Rohn said "You are the average of the five people you spend the most time with."

Complaining on things that are in his or her control, without any effort to make any change is a well-known characteristic of this average individual. This individual tends to blame others for his or her own mistakes.

Although this individual's thoughts-of-greatness is possible, he or she decides to not actualize those thoughts-of-greatness. This individual discourages others from actualizing their thoughts-of-greatness. He or she is fearful of the unknown, and succumbs to those fears. This individual looks for comfortability over progression and does not believe in mentors because he or she *knows-it-all.*

This average individual has many limiting beliefs and may understand he or she is average but does not search for methods to become preeminent. This individual lives a dull and mundane lifestyle and goes with the flow of the crowd. He or she may fool themselves in believing he or she is preeminent, and tends to procrastinate often.

This individual has many insecurities and does not accept constructive-criticism well. This individual understands effort towards his or her goals is gruesome work, and avoids challenges that are aligned with positive change.

Individuals in the **subpar success group** are usually unaware of which group he or she belongs to. A subpar individual will dislike his or her current situation within this current chapter in his or her life but this individual is too comfortable to progress and this individual does not seek to work towards any goal what so ever.

This individual usually has little to no control over his or her life as his or her life is being dictated by average people and/or preeminent individuals (e.g. employer, correctional officer, or manager, etc.).

He or she is limited in his or her ability to get out of the subpar success group and this individual may forever be a part of this group. This individual may be incarcerated, homeless, or a low-ranking employee. This individual could be handicap, disabled, unemployed, or mentally ill. He or she could be an impaired patient, and could be dumb and/or blind. Pay attention to the emphasis on the words "could be," as not everyone with those traits fit this group.

It is known, not all people who are incarcerated, homeless, low ranking employees, handicap, disabled, mentally ill, impaired, dumb, or blind are part of the subpar success group. It is very possible for these individuals to be part of the average success group and even possible for a minority of these individuals to be part of the preeminent success group.

Some characteristics of this individual is his or her finding of no pleasure in advancing in life. He or she will usually condemn his or herself to a small area in his or her city, town or state and have no thoughts or ambition of ever experiencing what life is like outside of the boundaries he or she has set for him or herself. This individual can find the negativity in any situation, positive or not. This individual may believe many people in the world has done some type of injustice in his or her life.

He or she may find imperfections in a lot of other people but will find him or herself perfect. This individual may steal or mooch resources such as money or food from others with no intent to repay. It may be difficult for him or her to adhere to policies, which may leave this individual unemployed or underemployed.

This individual's ability to learn has been self-terminated due to laziness and he or she will usually resort to violence to get his or her point across versus by conversation. This individual's ability to control his or her temperament and impulsivity, or self-control has been diminished and his or her reactions are based on emotion.

Your friends can only bring you out of one, and into one of the other two groups, up or down. There is no in between. In the event, you are in the average success group and are actively working on your thought-of-greatness, and your friends, verbal directors or indirect influencers are directly or indirectly keeping you in the average success group (95%), your friends, verbal directors, or influencers are bringing you Down.

If you are in the average success group and you are slowly working your way down to the subpar success group, and your friends, or influencers are working to keep you in the average success group, your friends, or influencers are bringing you Up.

If you feel your friends are neither bringing you Up or bringing you Down, **they are bringing you Down.** In this chapter, the meaning of bringing-you-down is your aid in moving you away from your actualization of your thoughts-of-greatness which is lived in the preeminent success group.

In most cases, you will find those individuals that neither brings you Up or Down, are a form of escapism. Their purpose in your life is to aid in your escapism. Anyone or anything that is not aiding in your achievement of your greatness is an anchor to your success and bringing you Down. Everyone in the subpar success group, who is not actively searching for a way out of that success group, is continually bringing everyone in that group, that is searching for their greatness, Down.

Without following the principles in this book, for individuals who work towards their thoughts-of-greatness, life can be a continuous travel between the three success groups. There are over 25 directions an individual can maneuver through the success groups and each direction will not be listed to determine if their friends, or influencers are either bringing them Up or Down.

In this chapter, the meaning of bringing-you-down is your aid in moving you away from your actualization of your thoughts-of-greatness. Individuals who bring you Up are individuals who aid in your movement towards actualization of your thoughts-of-greatness, which the actualization of your thoughts-of-greatness is experienced in the preeminent success group.

Are You Down With OPP?

You want to put yourself around **O**nly **P**ositive **P**eople, choose to put yourself around people who can help you actualize your thoughts-of-greatness. Your friends should Only be Positive People. Without burning any bridges, remove people who negatively affect your actualization of your thoughts-of-greatness.

Similar in my situation when I had to terminate my employee in the sub-chapter Termination of a Weak Link, you need to terminate some people in your life. And you already know who those people are.

One brilliant way of removing people from your life without burning a bridge is to drown them out with productivity. Become so productive in actualizing your thoughts-of-greatness that you truthfully do not have time to entertain negative people. Negative people are not only the individuals that say or do bad things to you, they are also the individuals that waste time and drain energy.

Time Wasters are one of the most negative types of people. These individuals are the copious amount of water from Chapter 3: Lead Your Life.

Excerpt from Chapter 3: Lead Your Life

> The current is attempting to bring you to the middle of the ocean where there is nothing but a copious amount of water that has no greater purpose in your life than to keep you in the middle of the ocean, until you die.

Look at life like a timeline. You have a beginning, a middle and an end. The beginning is your birth and your childhood. The middle is your young adult and adult stage; where you go to high school, college, and work. The end, is well you know... the end. If a person can waste as much time as they can, for the time that has been allotted for your life, they control how much of your thoughts-of-greatness you actualize or how many goals you complete. The more time that person wastes is less time you possess to actualize your thoughts-of-greatness.

When Time Wasters waste your time, do not take it personal, usually it is not to be malicious. It's usually simply because they are either average or subpar and are not following their own thoughts-of-greatness. They have a lot of time on their hands to waste and these individuals feel comfortable sharing that time with you. It is your responsibility to limit the time wasted. This rule also goes for Energy Drainers. An Energy Drainer will suck the energy out of you to affect your ability to put in work. Limit time spent with Energy Drainers as you would with Time Wasters.

Direct Mentorship

There is a way out of the average success group; there are actually dozens of ways out of the average success group. I will speak on the most effective strategy, which is direct mentorship. Mentorship is the relationship between a more experienced or more knowledgeable person that will help and lead a less experienced or less knowledgeable person.

Direct mentorship is the intimate relationship between a mentor and a mentee, where the mentee works directly with the mentor either in person or through means of conversation between the two individuals. The mentee should utilize the mentor as a tool, like a map, to direct and help him or herself to become part of the preeminent success group. Those who are preeminent can have mentors that will aid him or her higher in the group.

Following the instructions of a good mentor will help in building your confidence, aid in removing your limiting beliefs, shift your average habits to preeminent habits, help you in getting you to feel the good feeling of following your dreams, that will then trigger your natural trait for you to share the experience with others, which is your encouragement to other people to follow their dreams. Your mentor will teach you the importance of leading your life and much more, this will aid in your success of living your thoughts-of-greatness.

As for those who are interested in the monetary aspect of the preeminent success group; these characteristics are prerequisites for the attainment and maintenance of large sums of money. I will not discuss ways to go Down in the success groups as there are hundreds of ways to do it, also it won't be in the context of this book, in addition, it will not be to your benefit. Finding a mentor is not easy, nor is it extremely difficult. Here are a few simple steps can help you in finding a mentor:

1.   **Review your values of toil**, when seeking a mentor, your values of toil should be in checklist form. Aim to attract and/or find individuals that their values of toil are equal to or like your values of toil.

2.   **Reverse engineer** the person you want to become. Write down the characteristics of the person you want to be in the future. Think about the person you want to become and how does that person walk, work, talk, dress, and behave. Write this down in detail as it is imperative that you are as specific as possible. After writing the characteristics of this person, Visualize and think back, step by step as to what it is that you have to do to become this person. (e.g. I visualize a person with straight teeth, I need to get braces to be this person)

3.   **Research those characteristics** and learn to cultivate those traits on your own. Understand that a

mentor's job is only to guide you. You must do the work on your own. Learn the characteristics that you want to have, and put them to practice. Try your best; on your own, to create the person you want to become, the good mentor will construct your mistakes and flaws.

4.   **Actively Search** for people who match those characteristics, values of toil and live the lifestyle you are interested in living and who are currently living or have lived the thoughts-of-greatness you are having.

5.   **Do Whatever It Takes** to get this person to directly mentor you. Directly means you are working with this person either in person or through means of conversation, where the conversation is between you and the mentor. The bigger your thoughts-of-greatness are, the harder it will be to have a mentor of equivalence. However, whatever it takes means whatever it takes. One phone call, a knock on their door and an e-mail will usually not work.

A principle to understand is under the power of association. The people you connect with, your friends, acquaintances, and associates have the ability to help or hinder you in reaching your goals and becoming successful or not. People from a lower group will most of the time have little to no value to you besides escapism. Most of those in the preeminent success group understand this simple rule and are selective with the people they mentor.

Therefore, you must be willing to do whatever it takes to gain their mentorship. Doing whatever it takes will show the prospective mentor that you are serious about changing your life. You too are to be selective with whom you associate yourself with as they can either bring you Up or Down.

11

MANEUVER TO THE WEST

"Get out of your comfort zone, growth does not happen there."

—Andy Audate

Something in me was reminding myself about how fast the end of life comes; I knew at that point, I must make a choice, it is either now or never. The next day, I got into my car and drove to my longtime best friend, Patrick's house. I was standing while he sat down at the kitchen table. One afternoon on that late December day, while talking in his kitchen, I asked him a simple question, "Pat, what's going to happen differently in 2016 than what happened in 2015?" Patrick could not answer the question.

The way life was for us was that we partied when we could, wasted time searching for escapism through associates, and worked at our jobs. My purpose was slowly diminishing after learning that Progression Wireless was not truly what I wanted to do. At this point, I felt there was no reason for me to be in Rhode Island besides working at Progression Wireless.

But I can't do that; I can't stay in Rhode Island. I had a knot in my stomach feeling like I am wasting my life doing something that I do not want to do. Based on the definition of Lead and the standards it entails, I must lead my life and utilize my time the way I want to in its best manner that is aligned with my goals. At this time, my goals were not defined but I knew what my values of toil were, and I made a decision based on my values of toil.

I asked Patrick if he was open to doing "something crazy" in 2016. When I asked him that, he showed a face of curiosity with a smirk that showed his interest. As I smiled back, I was nervous to tell him what was on my mind. There was something that has been on my mind for years.

Since I can remember, living in California has always been a dream for me. When I did watch TV and I saw those reruns, I learned that most of the people I saw on TV were living in California or the TV show took place out of California. These individuals on my TV screen were happy, and looked fulfilled with their life. Even though I realized they were actors, these individuals were people that were living their thoughts-of-greatness, in my eyes.

Then I remembered the time I laid on the bed listening to that song… "once, I was seven years old…" I felt my life would be passing by me. I was literally deciding to leave my parent's home where I was making money from my business, where I was comfortable, leaving everything that I knew in Rhode Island to go to California, of course I got scared, I was nervous.

Let's Move

Patrick expressed to me his goals in music. He has wanted to be in the music industry for a long time now. The words came out of me, I said to Patrick, "Let's move to California." After those words left my lips, every second felt as long as a minute as I waited for his response. He looked away as he pondered on the idea. Time was going by too slow, so I quickly added that we could go there for just three months.

"We can go there for three months." I added that because although it was a great idea, fear came over me; I got nervous as I thought about what going to California would entail. I thought about all the negatives, I thought about going homeless, losing money, being the one to make the wrong decision, looking stupid to my peers, thinking about the financial responsibilities that I had in Rhode Island, I was not sure what would happen with my employees, I had no idea...

Instead of *moving* to California, I only wanted to go for three months. Three months was only ninety days. I told Patrick that we would still be in the year of 2016 if we left to California in March and came back to Rhode Island three months later in June, the adventure would not be that long. "Yeah, three months, that's not too bad" I said.

He agreed, this would just be a long vacation. At the time, I planned to run Progression Wireless from a distance, and Patrick would request three months off from his job. Patrick and I discussed shipping one car to Los Angeles, and we would share that car.

We figured out transportation but we did not figure out the housing. We searched and searched for housing that we can reside in for three months. During that three-month stay, we had requirements that we wanted to be met in the place we'd stay. Like myself, Patrick lived at home with his Mom and because leaving home for a long time was brand new to us, we wanted to be as comfortable as possible, even though it would only be for three months.

A few days later after making the decision to go to California for three months, Patrick met me at my house and we discussed what our ideal living situation would be like. We wanted to find a beautiful hardwood floored apartment with two bedrooms and two bathrooms with furniture already in the apartment in a similar price range of Rhode Island's rental market.

After researching online, I found that Los Angeles' rental market was nearly five-times the rent that was in Rhode Island. When I saw the rental rates, I called the apartment complexes to verify as I thought the rates on the website were incorrect, but when I called, I found out that it was correct. I was in awe. Just the high rental rates were a reason to stay in Rhode Island and not go to California. As I spoke to Patrick about the high rental rates, he reassured me that the rental rates were nothing we couldn't handle and we shouldn't decide to not go based on a dollar.

I had a thought-of-greatness about going all-in and completely moving to California. Deep inside, my dream was to live in California; I wanted to experience the feeling of happiness that I saw on those TV shows, but I was too scared to do it. This is the reason I suggested to Patrick we only go for three months.

Going to California for just three months was the safest way without going all-in on my dreams. Going to California for just three months would allow me to have a taste of my dreams. Fear held me back from going all-in and experiencing my dream of *living* in California. I decided to keep this trip a small vacation until Patrick brought up my dream.

Come to My House

Patrick sent me a text message in the middle of the night, he asked me to meet him at his house. I left my house and drove through the dark and rainy city of Pawtucket, to arrive at his house only a few minutes later. When I arrived, I sent Patrick a text message letting him know of my arrival. I pulled into his driveway and moments later he walked down his driveway and entered my car. I can tell he had something on his mind. I remained parked, and he explained to me that we needed to go all-in and move to California with no intention of coming back to Rhode Island.

We discussed our dreams and moving was aligned with my thoughts-of-greatness. With Patrick's support, I said, "Let's do it." After I agreed, fear was haunting me for days. I wanted to move to California, but I had an established business, established relationships with friends and I was scared to go all-in, but because I had a friend to push me to follow my dreams is an example of how friends can bring you up the success group.

Recap

Although deep down, I knew that I wanted to move to California and not visit for three months, I was planning to not go all-in out of fear. In this event, Patrick was a verbal director, he told me what I should do, and he told me to go all-in and move. Patrick was pushing me to follow my dreams and he would take the journey with me.

My feelings on moving slid between nervousness and

excitement. I was nervous for what I was about to go through and excited to experience a change that was in alignment with my thoughts-of-greatness.

Late at night, in my bed, before I went to sleep, I searched the Internet for videos on how life was like in California. Intrigued by the lives of other people that moved from their hometown to California, I watched Vlogs and read about the life I would soon live. I began to prepare my mind that in less than ninety days I would be a Californian. I prepared the Progression Wireless stores for complete closing.

At the time, I had two stores remaining, one in Massachusetts and the other in Rhode Island. The rental lease for the Massachusetts store was near its end, ending within twenty-five days. The Rhode Island store's lease would end within sixty-five days. Because of my decision to move to California, I did not renew either lease.

As weeks went by, the employees knew of my decision to move away. I did not want to affect their livelihood; I decided to help them as much as I could with their search in new employment. As days were passing, inventory was being sold and I was not reordering inventory.

Slowly but surely, inventory was being moved from the Massachusetts store to the Rhode Island store. On a dark and cold night, I had to visit the Massachusetts store to pick up inventory to transfer it to the Rhode Island store. I was with Patrick and he came along for the ride.

The Ride to the Store

On this ride, Patrick explained something that has been on his mind. He wanted to back out from moving to California. I was shocked and I asked why. He told me that his responsibilities in Rhode Island were keeping him there, his bills, his job, and his friendships. How is it possible that a few weeks prior he was ready to move, he was pushing me to move, then a few weeks later, he no longer wants to go.

I figured it out, doubt crept into his mind, and the reasons of why he shouldn't move was temporarily prioritized over reasons why he should move.

In the car, on our way to the Massachusetts store, I changed the conversation from reasons why he shouldn't move to California to reasons why he should. All he needed was one good reason to go and it should expunge every reason to not go. When we arrived to the Massachusetts store, Jarixa was working.

At the store, her, Patrick and I spoke about the perks of moving to California. There were more perks to move than to stay in Rhode Island. I explained to him that there were opportunities he may be missing out on if he stayed in Rhode Island, and he agreed. In one night, he went from his mind full with doubt and no longer wanting to go to California, to discarding all those negative thoughts and he made a decision to move.

After all of this, we had about eighty-five days left until it was time to move. Neither I or Patrick had told our parents about the plans to move to the West Coast. We felt we were old enough and we did not need to include them in on our plans. I can tell my mom was curious and was aware something was going on with the internet searches of California rent, with Patrick coming to the house and us talking about plans for California, but I didn't tell her that I was going, she just had assumptions.

Although we were planning to move, Patrick and I were still hanging out, partying and finding escapism in the people we hung out with. One day I went to Patrick's house to meet up with him. His mom, Monalisa, was home cooking some Cape-Verdean food. I walked into his house to find out Patrick had told his mom that we were moving. As I was walking into the house, she yelled "Andy... Why" multiple times.

All I could do was smile and say "Why what?" She did not understand the reasoning behind us wanting to move. Patrick and I explained our ideas on what could go right for us if we were in California, and we also explained our thoughts-of-greatness, but she did not see it this way; she just saw her son was planning to leave home and move away to the other side of the country.

Monalisa went on asking us where would we live and how would we support ourselves, and Patrick and I couldn't answer her questions. We simply did not know where we were going to live and how we would support ourselves. She never told us to not move, what she did do was make statements that would discourage of us from moving.

She asked me how much the rent was in California, I laughed because I didn't want to tell her the price of rent was nearly five-times the amount of Rhode Island's rent. And when I did tell her how much the rents were in California; she was quick to tell Patrick and I that for the two-bedroom and two-bathroom apartment we would be getting in California, we can pay much less for the same type of apartment in Rhode Island. I agreed with her about the rent but actualizing our thoughts-of-greatness were more important.

As any loving mother would, I understood, she did not want to see her son move across the country to an unfamiliar area. Mother's instinctively want to put their children in the least amount of danger, and because neither Patrick, myself, or Monalisa had been to California, every possible negative and positive experience ran through her mind. Shortly after, I ate some of the food Monalisa was cooking, then Patrick and I left the house to go on with our night.

Then a few days later, I told my mom and dad that I was going to move to California. Their reaction was subtle and their response was nonchalant. Days after days passed, and one day when I was home, I was on the home computer searching for Apartments for rent in California. My mom walked in from the kitchen to the living room, where the computer was and asked me a question and then told me a story. With a smile of curiosity, she asked me "What is so good in California that you want to go there?" I can tell this has been on her mind.

I replied to her "an experience." I was going to experience my thoughts-of-greatness. She then told me a story about a young man that she knew of, this young man left his home to go to California in pursuit of something he wanted to achieve. After not accomplishing anything for five years, this man returned to his parent's home. I had no clue why she told me that story, I understood it as her telling me there could be a possibility that I could have the same experience as that young man. This is an example of an Indirect Influence.

A few days after that, as I was cleaning my bedroom, in a calm tone, my dad came to speak to me. He sat me down on the side of my bed and asked me. He asked me to not go to California. I could not agree with him; I love my dad but little did he know I was actualizing my thoughts-of-greatness for him in addition to the rest of the individuals depending on me. I had been set on following my thoughts-of-greatness and I couldn't put that to the side to listen to my dad. This is an example of a verbal director.

I went back to focusing on closing Progression Wireless, I closed the Massachusetts store and transferred those employees to the Rhode Island store.

Days later, the time had passed and the time to move was here. Instead of shipping one car, Patrick and I shipped our cars to California. Three days after shipping my car, I got on a plane and flew to California.

The Epitome

Patrick has been my friend for over seven years, this is because he brings me towards being the best version of myself, he pushes me to go higher in the success group and so do I for him. When I was scared to go all-in on my dreams to live in California, Patrick was there to bring to light what I was hiding, which was my fear to go all-in. Instead of going to California and doing a three month stay because of my fear to go all-in, he pushed me passed my fears and brought them to light when he said we needed to go all-in and move to California. I was allowing fear to lead me and I was not leading my own life.

In another instance, when Patrick and I were going to the Massachusetts store, and right after telling me to go all-in and move, he explained to me that he wanted to back out of moving to California. Doubt had crept into his head and he became fearful as the date to move was getting closer and closer. Then I helped him overcome that doubt and aided him to actualize his thoughts-of-greatness.

Monalisa and my mom were both indirect influencers. Mothers naturally want to protect their children from danger and remove their children from harm's way.

Although they love us very much and were only trying to protect us. Because neither my mom or Monalisa had been to California, neither of them knew what life would be like there. Patrick's and my thoughts-of-greatness lied in California and with their indirect influence, they were attempting to keep us in Rhode Island.

They did not specifically tell us not to go to California, but they tried to persuade us to not go by attempting to shine light on our ignorance of where we would live, how we would support ourselves, and other areas. If either Patrick or I listened to our moms, we would have been imbalanced.

However, my dad was a verbal director, he specifically asked me to not go to California. There is a difference between an indirect influence and a verbal director.

Indirect influencers can influence you using non-verbal communication as well. In an example, if you tell someone you want to accomplish a goal and that person responds with an eye-roll, this is an example of an indirect influence. When that person does their eye-roll, you can see their reaction is in disbelief.

This disbelief from another person, if you agree with it, can cause an imbalance in you and effect you reaching your thoughts-of-greatness. A common indirect influencer's choice of words is "yeah right." This is when you tell a person your thoughts-of-greatness, and their response is "yeah right." I call them the **yeah-righters**. For these individuals live in the average success group or the subpar success group.

A close friend of mine was a yeah-righter, he thought Patrick and I were not serious when we said we were moving to California. It was not until we shipped our cars to California he then believed we were going. His disbelief in us was an indirect influence, had I believed in his disbelief, that would have put me in a place of imbalance.

Closing the business and moving to California has so-far been one of the best decisions I have made in my life. Had I continued to live in fear and only visit California for three months, I wouldn't have reaped the rewards I've received, as these rewards took place after living in California for six months.

Neither my mom, Patrick's mom, or my dad wanted me to go to California. My close friend doubted that Patrick and I were going to go. Listening to either of these individuals would have made me imbalanced and I would not have been actualizing my thoughts-of-greatness. The objective is to remain balanced in actualizing your thoughts-of-greatness.

12

THE NEXT MOVE

"All of us are winners, but some of us are producing results we don't want."

–Les Brown

There is something I know about you. Yes, You! The one reading this book. There is something I know about you. What I know about you is that you are rare and part of a rare breed. You realize that It's Not Ok to Be Average, and I appreciate that.

Out of millions and millions of sperm cells, you were *chosen*! You were chosen for a particular purpose, and this purpose has a massive impact on the world and many of the individuals that live in it. As there are many people living in the subpar success group and the average success group, It may be hard to believe that you were chosen. The question may arise, how or why me? Well, I can't answer the question "Why you?"

Sometimes, we as humans tend to limit what we think

we are capable of. You are capable of anything you set your mind to. This is not positive thinking bullshit, but factual information. As of today, not the day that I am writing this book, but the day you are reading it, there is someone and in many cases there are some people who are depending on you. You may have yet to know who those individuals are but they are faithfully depending on you.

These individuals need YOU and only YOU. The way to help them is to actualize your thoughts-of-greatness and become the best version of yourself, be The Real You and accept the responsibilities. What God has planned for your life will help those individuals but that's when you start to go towards you becoming The Real You.

As humans, negativity is usually prioritized over positivity in your mind. I want to share something with you, I have personally seen instances where individuals I have encountered have gone from a horrible chapter in their life to being fulfilled, happy and making that positive impact in the world because of their actualization of their thoughts-of-greatness.

What that looked like was an individual that was living with no hope on the brink of suicide to actualizing his thoughts-of-greatness through belief and the help of God. By actualizing his thoughts-of-greatness, he was able to help others help themselves.

Another example is Nicholas Vujicic. He is a motivational speaker and Christian evangelist born with tetra-amelia syndrome, a rare disorder that left him without legs or arms. A man that could have thought his life had little to no meaning decided to actualize his thoughts-of-greatness and by him doing so, he is pouring hope into individuals all over the world.

I've read online about people with disabilities that thank Nicholas for his courage to speak as he has helped those individuals overcome struggles in their lives. If Nicholas did not actualize his thoughts-of-greatness, who would have been there for those individuals? He accepted the responsibility.

Accept the responsibility for the people who depend on you. And do whatever it takes to make your thoughts-of-greatness come to fruition. This book was generalized for you to understand that in all and everything that you do, there is a level of averageness. You do not fit into that level of averageness.

With your belief and hard-work, you are preeminent and you set the level that others seek to work towards. But for that to happen, you must believe in it and you must work hard for it. This book was designed in a way that you can use these principles in all aspects of your life from school, to work, to family and relationships.

One Favor

I wrote this book to create a shift in this world and I need your help to make this impact. Here is part of your responsibility: **I thank you for you reading this book, but I need you to give this book away for free**. Think about one person who would benefit from the teachings of this book. Whoever that person is, without thinking if you should or should not, just do it, give this book as a gift to him or her after completing this chapter.

My goal is to have this exact copy of this book reach fifteen different owners throughout its life cycle. But I do have one rule that I ask that you follow. **Do not explain what you learned from this book to the person you are giving it to.**

The reason is because out of everything in this book that you read, there were one or two topics that you connected with. If you were to explain your connections in this book to that person, you will speak only on the one or two topics that *you* connected with. However, the person that's receiving this book may connect with another teaching and you could turn them off by your connections.

By following this rule, you truly do benefit the person and allow him or her to read this book with an open mind. Do not be selfish with the teachings of this book. The more people around you that know about the teachings, the better their lives become as they actualize their thoughts-of-greatness.

Because those individuals actualize their thoughts-of-greatness, with the power of association, you will move to a higher success group. It is a benefit to you and your thoughts-of-greatness that your friends and family members actualize their thoughts-of-greatness. To aid in their progress to a higher success group, tell them to get this book.

If someone is interested in reading this book, or is curious about this book and asks you what the book is about, have them read the introduction and at the end of reading the introduction, ask them if they want to continue to read it or not. If that person wants to continue reading, give them this book.

If you are the individual that received this book from another person for free, WOW! That person cares about you. Now it is your responsibility to do the same; give this book to the first person that pops in your mind, give it to them for <u>free</u>. Who do you know that could benefit from the teachings in this book? Give it to them.

No More Average

We were raised average; in first grade, you were taught to get in line, color in between the lines and not speak out loud but wait until called on after raising your hand. Everyone had to do this. I recall in middle school, when I received my report card, there were three tiers for the grading system: above average, average and below average.

First off, it is fascinating that all three tiers are based on average. The second thing, is when a student's grade fell below average, the parents were notified and the student had to work harder to get his or her grades up. However, when a student was average, the student was not reprimanded, and the parents were not notified. This was a conditioning of your mind that allowed your subconscious to believe it was ok to be average. The truth is that It's Not Ok to Be Average. As you grew older, you may have realized that your mind was being programmed to believe average was ok.

Many think life is like a game of chess. Life is actually like a game of checkers. Chess is too complicated and not too many people know how to play, but checkers on the other hand, many people know how to play and it's simple; this is true about life. Life is simple and many people, including you, know how to play. In checkers, when the opponent makes a move towards you, you must protect yourself to win.

However, the rule is you always have to move forward until your piece wins and you become King. When you are King, your moves can be forward and backward to help the others pieces on the board. In life, when you are King, you are no longer average. Therefore, because you are no longer average, you can go back to help others in actualizing their thoughts-of-greatness, this is your responsibility if you accept.

Life tends to make a move on you to win, you are worthy enough to beat life. Life is your bitch, and you demand what you want out of your life. Your life does not control you, unless you allow it to. In checkers, it is always the turn of one of the players. This time in your life, it's your turn. Make a move forward.

In the future, you are on your deathbed lying down with your eyes glued to the ceiling. Literally, you are on your deathbed. Death is around the corner; any minute, any hour, any day now, it is soon to be your time. What is the conversation you have with yourself?

It is either based on one of the two: you realized you lived your life as The Real You or you lived your life as The Unfulfilled You. Were the responsibilities to live life as The Real You met?

#**NO**MORE**AVERAGE**

Quotes To Live By

There was a major shift in my life because of one quote; a few words in a short sentence can change your life's direction and reveal your purpose.

Inspirational quotes are important because they can activate your emotions in your mind and heart. The right quote can help you to see sunlight on a cloudy day and give you hope when things are getting rough.

Quotes can tell a story or an idea with your imagination. Here are some quotes to reflect on:

"You cannot change the people around you, but you can change the people you choose to be around." –Unknown

"Don't be a follower, be a leader." –Mike Desronvil

"We don't have control over time but we have control over what we do with our time." –Andy Audate

"All of us are winners, but some of us are producing results we don't want." –Les Brown

"There are three types of people in this world. Firstly, there are people who make things happen. Then there are people who watch things happen. Lastly, there are people who ask, what happened?" –Steve Backley

"If you don't help yourself, you become a burden to society." –Rob Tamboia

"It ain't how hard you hit, it's how hard you can get hit and keep moving forward." –Sylvester Stallone

"There are only two options: Make progress or make excuses." –Unknown

"Sometimes things fall apart so that better things can fall together." –Marilyn Monroe

"KIM! Keep It Moving." –Andy Audate

"Whatever the mind can conceive and believe, it can achieve." –Napoleon Hill

"We are all self-made, but only the successful will admit it." –Earl Nightingale

"You miss 100 percent of the shots you don't take." –Wayne Gretzky

"The key is to learn how to learn." –Andy Audate

"A dream written down with a date becomes a GOAL. A Goal broken down into steps becomes a PLAN. A Plan backed by ACTION makes your dreams come true." –Greg Reid

"It's Possible." –Les Brown

"Not only is it possible, it is necessary." –Les Brown

"Be obsessed with improvement." –Eric Thomas

"We must be able to control the controllable and be nimble to the things we don't have control over." –Andy Audate

"Be obsessed or be average." –Grant Cardone

"No truly great person ever thought themselves so." –William Hazlitt

"I fear all we have done is to awaken a sleeping giant and fill him with a terrible resolve." –Isoroku Yamamoto

"If you don't like something, change it. If you can't change it, change your attitude. Don't complain." –Maya Angelou

"I may have been born like this, I may have been created to be like this, but I am who I am because I am like this." –Andy Audate

"All your ideas may be solid or even good, but you have to Actually EXECUTE on them for them to matter." –Gary Vaynerchuk

"When you want something out of life, you've got to be willing to go into action, don't wait around for things to be just right, don't wait for things to be perfect, don't wait for the ideal situation, it will never be ideal." –Les Brown

"It's not hard to make decisions when you know what your values are." –Roy E. Disney

"Get out of your comfort zone, growth does not happen there." –Andy Audate

Acknowledgments

First and foremost, Thank You God for the breath in my lungs and the person you have made and allowed me to become. I would like to acknowledge and thank Gina and Bonaventure, Alain, Jorge Castillo, Joseph Jerez, Paulo Chavez, Jarixa Ramirez, and all former employees for your time invested in Progression Wireless.

Thank you Aziz M., for waking up the Sleeping Giant in me. Thank you Grandma, Grandpa, Monalisa, James J., Rosemary P., Keith M. and Mike C. Thank you to my high school teachers that either said or thought I would be a failure in life. Thank you Patrick Cardoso, for taking the leap of faith with me and constantly reminding me that what I set my mind to, is possible. Thank you Les Brown, Manny Barros, Eric Stoller, Marcos Orozco, Mike Desronvil, Scott B., Ona Brown.

Thank you to all who believed in me and in my ability to add positivity to the world. Thank you, the supporter and the reader of No More Average, thank you for reading my ideas, my experiences and utilizing the principles in your life.

Photo: ReneeFarias.com

Andy Audate is widely recognized as an eminent speaker with a delivery that is high energy and human potential stimulating. Raised in a low income city, a college dropout with little formal education; Andy took a path of entrepreneurship, forcing a course of endless self-education that has amounted to his successes. This path has not only allowed him to change his circumstance but allowed him to effectively communicate the desire to be great to others.

More at AndyAudate.com

GIFT THIS BOOK

TO:

FROM:

WOULD YOU LIKE ME TO COACH YOU, ONE-ON-ONE?

WITH PROVEN STRATEGIES I WILL AID & PUSH YOU TO ACTUALIZE YOUR THOUGHTS-OF-GREATNESS

WE'LL WORK TOGETHER

ANDYAUDATE@GMAIL.COM
PHONE: (323) 673-8876

RE: Message to You

Dear Sir or Madam:

God will Bless You on Your Journey. Every day, when you wake up, you must remind yourself. No More Average. You were not born average! You will not die average!

Best Regards,

Andy Audate

71984003R00083

Made in the USA
Columbia, SC
09 June 2017